THE SLOW ROAD NORTH

ALSO BY ROSIE SCHAAP

Becoming a Sommelier

Drinking with Men: A Memoir

THE
SLOW
ROAD
NORTH

How I Found Peace in an

Improbable Country

ROSIE SCHAAP

MARINER BOOKS

NEW YORK   BOSTON

HarperCollins books may be purchased for educational, business, or sales promotional use. For information, please email the Special Markets Department at SPsales@harpercollins.com.

FIRST EDITION

Designed by Chloe Foster

Library of Congress Cataloging-in-Publication Data
has been applied for.

ISBN 978-0-358-09745-7

24 25 26 27 28 LBC 5 4 3 2 1

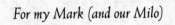

For my Mark (and our Milo)

THE SLOW ROAD NORTH

Prologue

A LONG MILE SOUTHEAST OF THE VILLAGE OF GLEN-arm, on the Antrim Coast Road, in the province of Ulster, there stands by the sea a monument to grief. It is not there in remembrance of the nearly one million people who died on this island during the famine in the middle of the nineteenth century, nor of the thousands of lives that were ended, or otherwise shattered, not so long ago, during the thirty years of violent conflict called the Troubles. It is a natural formation of stacked limestone boulders, something like an archway, with a large aperture near its center. A local landmark, it's known as the Madman's Window.

This is the story I have heard: Long ago, a woman died at sea, in the waters onto which the window gives view. There was a man who loved her, who would not accept that she was dead. From the day she went missing until his own death, he gazed through that stony window every day, hoping he would catch sight of her out there on the sea, alive, alive and calling for him. And when he saw her, he would jump into those cold waters, and bring her back to shore, back to him.

It was against reason, an act of wishful thinking. An act of grief wanting to be something other than grief. There were many deaths at sea in this part of the world. Everyone else knew that the woman he loved was dead, and they believed he had gone mad. If he was a madman, it is because loss had led him to despair. It is because without the one he loved, he could not be whole, could not even imagine it. Because grief, I know, can drive us mad.

1

DAY OF LOVE AND LOVERS, OF HEARTS AND ROSES red! Is Geoffrey Chaucer, the great poet-pilgrim of medieval England, to blame for this? Some say so: that it was he who transformed the ordinary enough feast day of an ordinary enough saint (what business does a saint have with all this hearts-and-roses stuff, anyway?) into a festival of courtly love. The association of February 14 with romance may have hatched about halfway into Chaucer's poem "The Parliament of Fowls," with these lines: *For this was on Seynt Valentines day/Whan every foul cometh ther to chese his make.* Saint Valentine's Day—when every bird comes to choose his mate.

On Valentine's Day, 2010, I lugged all five pounds and four ounces of my old college copy of *The Riverside Chaucer* to the room in a Brooklyn, New York, hospice where Frank, my mate of thirteen years, husband for seven, lay dying. But he did not lie, really: he revolved with effort to one side, flipped sharply on the other like a fish pitched ashore, and then, with resignation, rotated himself flat onto his back again, back to where he'd started. And again. He squeezed the white plastic button that permitted him to activate the pump that pushed opioids into his bloodstream when he needed them. He was forty-two.

There was little relief left for his bones and joints, his limbs and ligaments, but his mind was still alight with curiosity, still glimmering, more votive than bonfire now. His imagination, and that pulsing knot of muscle that is Saint Valentine's emblem: they were still active, and he was still yearning, even adrift on a plain of poppies. So, he—we—persisted in marking the day with our yearly tradition: reading "The Parliament of Fowls" aloud, each taking three stanzas before yielding to the other. If Chaucer really was behind all this, we had agreed long ago to surrender the day, or at least some good portion of it, to him, with pleasure. We liked to think we weren't corny (ha!)—especially Frank, who was always much cooler than me, a pretty low bar he cleared like a high jumper. He was an indie-rock, punk-rock kind of guy. I was an unreconstructed late-model folkie hippie.

Frank outstretched an arm to reach for his glasses on the night-stand and put them on: professorial but not prim, smart, with muddy-creek brown-green frames and glass trapezoids for lenses. An artist friend who had a day job at an optometrist's helped him pick them out. (I kept them for a very long time. They were one of Frank's totems, like the cast-iron skillet he cooked with almost every day for, what, fifteen years? Twenty? Since before we met. I kept that for a long time, too).

I held the Chaucer book open in front of him; he did not have the strength to support it. Neither of us could remember how long we'd been doing this, reading this long poem together on this day. Neither of us felt much but contempt for Valentine's Day—commercial! sexist! nonsense!—before the tradition began. I'm a

Capricorn, he was a Capricorn, and Capricorns don't do that sort of thing (he'd cringe if he heard me say this—because Capricorns don't do this sort of thing, either). He was an English professor; I wanted to be a poet; this was the kind of thing that could happen. And if any time was the right time to perform our most insufferably earnest selves, without shame, this was it.

But even reading—high on his list of loves, up there with our cats, cheese, punk rock, France, baseball, me—had become difficult to focus on. Still, he wanted to go on reading because he wanted to go on living. He was not one of those people who say they are ready for death. Can those people be serious? There were still too many books Frank wanted to read.

"*The lyf so short, the craft so long to lerne,*" I started, then caught my breath. How had I not thought about this first line, Chaucer's Middle English version of Hippocrates's *ars longa, vita brevis* (art is long, life is short), after so many readings of the poem?

Life is short: there, in that hospice room, it wasn't like we needed a medieval English poet or an ancient Greek physician to remind us so. But after almost two years of the ministrations of oncologists, endocrinologists, gastroenterologists, and surgeons; emergency room doctors, intensive care nurses, chemotherapy and radiation and PET scan technicians; a lay Jesuit chaplain-philosopher, a hugging saint from India, and a purveyor of medical marijuana—there was room for Chaucer and Hippocrates, too, and they took their places, as rightful as anyone else's, among all of those angels of life and death.

We sprinted—life *is* short—through the poem's long prefatory warmup, then slowed down to luxuriate in Chaucer's catalog of birds (*The peacock, with his angels feathers bright! The popinjay, full of delicacy!)* and the self-conscious enchantments of stanzas 53 and 54. *What should I say?* the poet asks at the start of 53, and I imagine two fingers pulling at a pointed beard, I infer a silent *hmm*. Stanza 54 begins with *But to the point*, and the reader wonders: Wait, there's a point? And does it matter?

"Pull yourself together, man," I said, to Chaucer, not to Frank, but to make Frank laugh, which he tried to do: a wrinkle tugged at the corners of his lips, at the edges of his drowsy blue eyes.

Soon came the single moment I love most: when the goddess Nature herself kisses with tenderness the beak of the lady eagle she holds on her hand, and who is central to the rest of the poem's action. Frank got this far maybe only to indulge me—even with the pain, the bullying pain that would not be subdued, even with the drugs, he remembered it's my favorite part. But then, he had to sleep, or at least try to sleep. Maybe we would read the rest later. Maybe we wouldn't: art is long.

In the afternoon, Frank sighed and rumbled in and out of sleep, while I sat in the chair beside his bed. I thought about him, and his suffering, and I considered the poignancy of his optimism, which hadn't flagged until these final few days. If anything good can be said about his cancer, it's that it hadn't caused excruciating pain until it spread to his pancreas not long before he died. He had taught his last class only yesterday, online, a little loopy with meds, but he wanted to be with his students. We were both teachers when we met.

I thought about our marriage: when it was good, and when it

was not. I thought about my mother, who was also dying, but not so soon: she had been dying for a long time. I thought about bills. And changing the cat litter. And taking out the recycling. And I thought about Ireland—because it was there, long ago, that I met Saint Valentine.

I made my first trip to Ireland in the summer of 1991, when I was twenty, because of another poet: William Butler Yeats. I wanted to study his poetry in Dublin, where he was from. But lectures at Trinity College tumbled swiftly from the top of my priority list; within a week, they foundered far below the other pleasures that had revealed themselves to me: long afternoons and evenings at my favorite pub, and another blue-eyed man I loved, who had had cancer, too.

One afternoon, when I'd strayed only blocks from my usual circuit, the terrain grew unfamiliar. I kept walking: unknown streets were interesting streets. I stopped in front of a grim, gray building, as practical and unadorned as a small fort. It was Whitefriar Street Church, dedicated to Our Lady of Mount Carmel—the Virgin Mary in her persona as patroness of the Carmelite Order.

Curiosity drew me into its sanctuary. Much better inside: pale as thick cream, cool, calm, clean, quiet. And, there to one side as I walked in the direction of the altar: a shrine to Saint Valentine. What was he doing here? In a marble alcove in the wall, above a side altar, his likeness in statue stood barefoot, draped in red vestments, clutching in one hand a crocus. Below the altar: a casket, inside which were swaddled the saint's remains, or some of them, anyway, taken there in the 1830s by an Irish Carmelite named John Spratt. So admired was Spratt for both his homiletic virtuosity and his care for the poor people of Dublin that Pope

Gregory XVI himself saw fit to confer upon him Saint Valentine's relics as a token of his esteem. The inscription: *This shrine contains the sacred body of Saint Valentinus the Martyr, together with a small vessel tinged with his blood.*

So grave, so serious! But I found it funny, too: another example of the habitual, sometimes charming, sometimes exasperating strain of embellishment I'd grown accustomed to from Dubliners I knew. There had to be other sites that claimed to be Saint Valentine's final resting place. But something, some softening, made me lower my shield of skepticism, and let Dublin have it: here, in this gray everyday church in this gray everyday city that had come to feel like home to me, among its public houses and two-story brick terraces, its low, impassive office blocks and bookmakers' storefronts, rested the priestly Roman prince of love himself.

Then a disordered reel of memories from that summer: a comic drama starring some stern goats on a beach in Sligo, a rave in the Wicklow Mountains, a lonely ride to a place I was told I should not visit, a kiss beneath the Spanish Arch in Galway.

Frank had never been to Ireland, but had wanted to visit—he loved Yeats, too, and Joyce, and part of his doctoral dissertation was about George Bernard Shaw—which, in that hospice room with no time left, felt unjust. But I might as well admit right now that there was a part of me—a shameful part where generosity falters—that had wanted to keep Ireland for myself, as if that were possible.

When Frank woke up, my thoughts of Ireland faded, and my attention snapped back to him. It was not time for Chaucer again: Frank was too tired, too restless, too aching. That Valentine's Day, we would not get to the end of the poem. Instead, we had the 2010 Winter Olympics, in Vancouver, for our evening's entertainment. I went out to buy milkshakes from the Baskin-Robbins ice cream shop around the corner from the hospice: strawberry for him, mint chocolate chip for me. Frank, the best home cook I've ever known—he of the New Year's Eve cassoulet that took a week or more to coax and caress into being, the pork and pistachio terrines and duck rillettes and choucroute garnie, all of which had often made me refer to him as my French farm wife (which he knew I meant as praise), whose rare splurges were on special-occasion dinners at restaurants beyond our means—only wanted ice cream. Who wouldn't?

We toasted "Happy Valentine's Day" with our milkshakes and sipped them while we watched the women's speed skating in quiet awe—those lean, powerful bodies crouched nearly parallel to the ice, the blades of their skates like cleavers poised at the close, correct angle against a sharpening steel. We coasted into sleep with the television on, and neither of us slept well.

It was not until early morning that Frank fell into a deep sleep. After twenty-four hours at his bedside, I left the hospital and went home, just a few subway stops away, to take care of a few errands. I shoved an arbitrary armful of laundry into our landlady's washing machine; she let me use it that week, knowing that Frank was in hospice and there was no time for a laundromat. I fed and petted and talked to our cats: a silver tabby I'd raised since she was weaned, and an ancient rescued tortoiseshell whom Frank and I re-rescued from my mother when she could no longer care for her. I had paid them too little attention lately, but because they loved him, too, I assured myself that they would understand. I thanked them for their patience and asked for their pardon. I scrolled through a week's worth of emails. I wrote a message to Frank's far-flung family. These were not the words I used, but this was what they meant: *Get here. Now.*

A short shower. A glance at our bed: not a chair in a hospice room, our bed, with our frayed flannel sheets as soft and fuzzy as lamb's ears, and what Frank always thought was an overabundance of pillows, especially because I tossed most of them to the floor before going to sleep. It would only be a quick nap, half an hour at most. I sank into it.

When I woke up, it was after noon.

What have I done?

I had missed him by minutes.

A nun, the hospice chaplain, stood in front of the closed door to his room. She wouldn't let me in, wouldn't let me see him. I shouldn't have gone home. I shouldn't have slept.

I collapsed to the linoleum floor. I screamed and sobbed at the same time—is that what wailing is? had I wailed?—and the nun shushed me so I would not disturb the other patients, the other families. I had soaked my green woolen cardigan with tears, and the dampness drew from its fibers a sour, lanolin smell.

She shushed me again. She was small, and old, but strong

enough to hoist me to my feet, lead me into her office, deposit me in a stiff chair like a sack of groceries, and pull the door shut behind us.

"He was afraid," she told me, as though candor is always for the best. I hated her more than I had ever hated anyone in my life.

I thought of Frank, alone with only *this person* at his side. Alone, and afraid, just like she said. I considered the miserable truths she might have felt obligated to tell him out of her commitment to honesty, and I pictured him again: alone, afraid, then gone. When he needed me most, I was not there, and for that selfishness and carelessness, I could not be forgiven.

Were his glasses on? Where was his wedding band?

What did she say to him?

Had I kissed him before I slipped out of the room that morning? What were our last words to one another? Had they had been "Happy Valentine's Day," said for the fourth or fifth time in as many hours?

I hoped they had been "I love you."

Friends met me at the hospice, took me home, bought me dinner. My brother came down from Connecticut. Frank's parents drove straight through the night from West Virginia, fueled, I imagined, by anguish. What next? Them; me; a meeting in a funeral parlor.

I had never planned a funeral. I knew I wanted Frank to be buried at Green-Wood Cemetery—a beautiful and historic "suburb for the dead," the final resting place of Jean-Michel Basquiat, Louis

Comfort Tiffany, Lola Montez, many fallen Union soldiers—less than ten minutes' walk from home. A place we had visited together often, a place we both loved. I asked the memorial counselor—I think that's what he was called—at the cemetery if he could recommend a funeral parlor. He said he wasn't allowed to do that, and handed me a list of local ones. My eyes fell on what I took to be a Polish name—and my logic, because I knew no other logic for such circumstances, went like this: the neighborhood had a big Polish population in the 1950s and '60s, so this one had to be at least that old, and therefore experienced.

Frank's parents and I got to the funeral home a few minutes early. A friendly, dark-haired woman invited us to sit down on the couches in the lobby, which were arranged around a coffee table with a large artificial floral arrangement in a bowl-shaped vase at its center. I sat on one couch, my in-laws sat on the other, and from where I sat I thought I saw a can of cat food tucked next to the vase, only partly concealed by a cascade of fake blossoms. I looked again—yes, it *was* a can of cat food—and said nothing. I had picked this place, this funeral home with a can of Friskies Chicken and Salmon Dinner in Gravy on the table. What would Frank's parents think? Could they see it, too?

The funeral director emerged from her office and joined us. Doris looked to be nearly six feet tall, but at least four inches of that height came from her high heels, and maybe another three from her platinum updo. By then her dark-haired assistant had sat beside me. Doris greeted all of us, with the most beautifully gravelly, Brooklyn-y voice I'd heard in the many years I'd lived in the borough, and then settled in next to me on the other side of the couch, so that I was flanked by the two women I'd only just met.

When I made the appointment, I told the assistant the story of Frank's death. That he was young, too young. That he had borne his cancer ordeal with courage, even optimism. That all of this—burying a husband, planning a funeral, being a widow—was new to me.

Doris threw one of her arms around my shoulders; it ended with long and darkly polished, manicured nails. I turned my head to face her, and with a surprising intensity, our eyes met. Under all the mascara and all the eyeshadow, her eyes shone with compassion.

"Honey, I understand," she said in her sandpaper voice. "I understand. I have some idea how you're feeling. I also lost *my guy* when he was too young."

We nodded at one another with empathy and fellow feeling, eyes still locked; I did feel like she understood.

"His name was Guy," she added, with a shrug.

Frank's parents stayed mostly silent throughout, still suspended in the haze of heartache. Doris and her assistant and I talked through the burial and funeral plans. And then, when the clock struck noon, as though arriving at its usual appointed hour, a cat appeared on the sidewalk, just outside the glass front door. Doris's assistant retrieved the can from under the floral centerpiece, pulled off its lid, walked to the door, opened it, fed the cat, and returned to our meeting. She said nothing, and neither did the rest of us.

I couldn't tell if my in-laws had even noticed. I had—and I wanted to laugh, not only at the surreal weirdness of it, but also because of its matter-of-fact kindness. But something told me I could not laugh at anything, not at this, not now. Because it might upset Frank's parents—good people, generous people, people I loved, who were suffering beyond suffering. And because, no, it just wasn't right to laugh after one's husband had just died, alone, at age forty-two. It wouldn't be right.

A phone call with my mother, who was sorry she was not well enough to come to the funeral.

"It would be too much," I told her. "Just promise me *you* won't die this year."

The Vermont granite we chose for his headstone.

A green sprawl of cemetery.

A memorial in its gothic jewel-box chapel, where I decorated the altar with thin white tulips and the dollhouse daffodils of early spring. The tulips for the happy year Frank had lived in the Netherlands as a child, the daffodils because of Wordsworth. Doris, the funeral director, pulled up outside the chapel in her purple Cadillac convertible, marched down the aisle in her black suit and high heels, and placed an enormous spray of gladioli in front of the altar. They were at odds with the subtlety I had aimed for—but so what? She didn't have to come to the service; she was there for me, and I was glad to see her. Later, at the reception, I would hear that some people thought she might have been Frank's mistress—his glamorous, mysterious mistress—and I wished I could tell Frank, who would have laughed, and would have loved it, and would have dropped his jaw the way he did, he really did, when he heard something wonderful and outrageous.

I read Keats's nightingale ode (*thou wast not born for death!*), and had something like an out-of-body experience, the poem overtaking me when I could not find my own language, could not marshal my own emotions. Frank's father delivered a eulogy in a broken voice (he was not born to bury his child).

A reception at a restaurant in our neighborhood: pierogi and blini made with care by a chef who loved him, his favorite song by his favorite band (Minutemen's "History Lesson Part II"—*punk rock changed our lives*) strummed and sung by friends who loved him, too.

And when all that was done, an unending procession of paperwork, condolence cards, death certificates, deeds, contracts, bills. The weeks I spent in bed, flanked by cats, propped up on a pile of pillows, unable, or unwilling—not bothering—to get up, going nowhere.

Reentry came in stages: unsteady, slow, episodic. I took a trip to New Mexico over Passover, planned in a rare moment of clarity and calm, that had supplied a dramatic, welcome change of scenery—a breathing blanket of desert, a night sky like an indigo drop-cloth spattered with beads of paint, the rusty peaks of the Sangre de Cristo mountains like embers smoldering in the distance—and the soothing companionship, and home cooking, of old friends.

When I got back to Brooklyn, I picked up a day shift at a bar, fifteen years after I thought I'd left bartending for good, and it guaranteed that at least once a week, I had to shower, and brush my hair, and talk to people—things that no longer felt like ordinary, daily obligations to one's self and to others, but like honest achievements, small victories of will.

That summer, of all things, the World Cup gave me as good a reason as any to start writing again (I hadn't in months), and I blogged in exultation every time Holland won a game, and then another, and another, until they lost an ugly final match to Spain. My team had not won, but the tournament had given me a month-long furlough from despair, and what more could I ask of a sporting event? When it made me think of Frank—and it often did, since we had watched together in 1998, 2002, 2006 . . . was that all? a relationship of thirteen years spanned only three World Cups?—those thoughts were light, happy, unburdened.

Slow and unsteady, I was returning to myself—what else could I do?—but it wasn't the same self it had been before Frank got sick; I was a new and different me, whom I sometimes had to strain to recognize. To be a widow at thirty-nine is to be pitiable and pitied, and, in a sense, to be sanctified by misfortune: to be made into something else, someone else, different and set apart from others, automatically and undeservingly seen as saintly, but also as suspect. It is unnatural.

Call me not Naomi, the young widow commands in the Book of Ruth. *Call me Mara, for the Almighty hath dealt very bitterly with me.* Mara, the new name she gave herself, is a way of saying "bitterness" in Hebrew, but it also carries a suggestion of strength. I was gathering strength, but I was haunted by Frank's death, by my absence at the end of his life, by the ways in which I had failed him, and failed our marriage. The arrow of my bitterness was trained not on God, not on other people, not even on death: it was aimed at me, and I alone was its bull's-eye.

In October, obeying only an instinct—*life is short*—I went to Europe. The trip would take me to England and Germany—and Ireland. My last visit there, in 2008, had been practical: a research trip to Dublin for the book I was writing then, a week structured so that I could retrace steps I'd taken in the summer of 1991, find out where my memory had worked and where it had misled me, then correct myself, and my pages. This time, I had no agenda at all. Almost.

The plain gray church in Whitefriar Street had no place in my research two years earlier, no part in the story I needed to tell then. So much had changed: I had to see it again. The building looked less grim, less forbidding to me now, and, like the city of Dublin itself, much smaller. Inside, the saint's statue and shrine were as I remembered them: red vestments, crocus, casket, inscription. I stood before the shrine, and I waited. A few minutes, then a minute longer.

Nothing.

I felt only the familiar self-consciousness of being a Jew in a Catholic church, a scenario I'd been in many times before. But this time I wasn't in a Catholic church for a wedding, or a funeral mass, or to gape at a Caravaggio, or to tell the struggling members of a poor congregation how they could get food stamps and free legal assistance, as I often had when I was a community organizer a decade earlier. I was there because I wanted something for myself. But whatever that was, it was not forthcoming.

I could bear it no more than another minute when two lines from "The Parliament of Fowls" found their way to the tip of my tongue, late lines Frank and I had not reached in our final, halted attempt to read the poem together: *Saint Valentine, that art ful heigh on lofte/Thus singen smale fowles for thy sake.* Chaucer's words charmed me, as always. Frank, or some spirit of Frank, was by my side; but when was he not? There was no new feeling. No reward for my pilgrimage, if that was what this was. What had I expected? What had I wanted to feel? I didn't know, and it would not be forced.

But even if little, next to nothing, had happened at Saint Valentine's shrine, one thing was clear: Ireland was where I had to be. I had stayed in touch with my closest, oldest friends in Dublin; they knew that Frank, whom they'd never met, who was my husband and had been sick, was dead. At Philip's kitchen table, at a café with Nicole, I talked about him for hours, and they listened. And asked questions. And, sometimes, even smiled. And joked.

It wasn't that my friends in New York hadn't cared—they looked after me, and cooked for me, and they, too, had listened when I had to talk—but there was something different about the conversations with my friends in Ireland: a quality of acceptance, a directness, interest—sympathy unburdened by pity. Laughter was part of our conversations, too: a reprieve from the obligatory solemnity of bereavement I felt was required of me back home (whatever else we Americans are or are not, in this way our Puritan roots still show). Here, in Dublin, my widowhood seemed to define me no more nor less than anything else, and did not render me abject. For the many kindnesses given to me by my friends and family in New York, the same had not always been true there.

Ireland has its own ways with mourning, and with mourners. I felt it in Philip's clear-eyed openness at his kitchen table, and in Nicole's full, attentive presence at the café. I had some sense of this from the few wakes I'd been to, but I had not foreseen that it would be extended to me, and that it might start to clear a path toward a grief I could live with, maybe even live in, not postpone or push away.

In Dublin, I had been awakened to this possibility. But it wasn't until a few days later, after a quiet two-and-a-half-hour train ride to a place I'd been told to stay away from long ago, that I disembarked in a city whose intimacy with grief was painted on its walls and lodged in its cobblestones. In a country striving day after day to surmount sorrows of its own, I intuited that this might be the Ireland where I could tend to my sorrows, the Ireland I needed most. By then the path had cleared enough that I could see it was not directionless, and that my compass pointed north.

2

FLIGHT IS MY HABITUAL RESPONSE TO UNHAPPINESS—
maybe a bad one, and, often, in my case, an irresponsible one. This
is why, and how, I found myself in Belfast eight months after Frank
died, in autumn, 2010. If the choice was between fight and flight,
I could not fight grief. Grief, I thought then, will always prevail. I
would go away for two weeks, and I would try to leave it behind,
knowing that it would be right where I'd left it, waiting for me,
when I returned home.

I went to some familiar cities—London and Dublin, where I
had friends (and Saint Valentine) to visit—and to some less familiar ones, too. I hadn't traveled solely for pleasure since I was in
my late twenties: the precarious economics of life as a freelancer
made it impossible. Instead, before each trip, I would think up a
story to pitch, hopeful that I would at least break even in the end.
So on that same trip along with London and Dublin, I would also
go to Frankfurt, when its huge annual international book fair—
the Frankfurter Buchmesse—was on. Every year, one country is
chosen as the book fair's "Guest of Honor," and that year it was

Argentina. There were rumors that Argentina's greatest soccer players—Diego Maradona and Lionel Messi—would appear, and I thought there might be a story there, a fun story, about the collision of the genteel world of book publishing and the blazing international superstardom of football heroes.

Maradona and Messi didn't show up. I had no story to write, but my Frankfurt visit was not without pleasures: there was Feinstaub, a superb punk-rock bar close to where I was staying, and there was also the birthplace and boyhood home of Johann Wolfgang von Goethe—or, anyway, a reconstruction of it, as the original had been destroyed in the Second World War. Still, I knew that he had been born on that spot and had also written *The Sorrows of Young Werther* there, and that was enough; my emotions have always been susceptible to historic sites connected to writers I love, so Goethe and I had a moment in Frankfurt, *mehr licht!*

The first time I'd been to Germany was with Frank, in 1998. His parents were living in Bayreuth for a year, and, thanks to neighbors who'd become friendly with them, we were lucky to get tickets to a dress rehearsal of *Das Rheingold* at the opera house Wagner had designed himself. An austere hall, it has no center aisles—if someone seated in the middle must get out, it would be a long tight squeeze past endless pairs of knees. We had heard the story, long in circulation and probably untrue, that a man had died there about three hours into a production of *Die Meistersinger von Nürnberg*—Wagner's longest opera—and that his body stayed in its seat until the performance had ended. When Frank and I found our seats before *Das Rheingold*, we looked at each other and said, in unison, "don't die"—a decade before the possibility of Frank's death would become too real for even the lightest gallows humor.

In Frankfurt I felt his presence strongly, and for the first time, but not the last, I had the uncanny sensation that some of my decisions were somehow directed, if not by him, by my memories of him. When we met, a dark, loud punk rock bar would have been much more his kind of thing than mine. As much as I loved Goethe's poems in translation, Frank knew them better, and could read them in German.

I stayed in Nordend, a neighborhood of elegant buildings and boulevards lined with trees, in the spotless, minimalist apartment of a friend's sister and architect brother-in-law, equipped with an industrial espresso machine so big and shiny and red it resembled a small fire engine. I ate my fill of *würst*, and drank good, cold steins of beer—which Frank also would have loved. I walked the city's streets without a map, long before I had a smartphone, just rambling until something caught my attention and made me stop and look. It was a welcome kind of disorientation. For a city about which I'd heard almost nothing good—it was boring, people had told me, a business town, "like Hartford, but in German," in the uncharitable words of one friend—I'd found Frankfurt charming. It was greener than I'd expected, walkable, calm (compared to New York, anyway). But I suspect that those flashes of Frank's presence had also formed my good impression of the city.

Belfast was another city I hadn't often heard praised, but it, too, was on my itinerary. It was not as new to me as Frankfurt; I'd been there once, briefly, when I was a student in Dublin. Back then, I had gone, really, for only one reason: because I was told not to.

The paternalistic powers-that-be who supervised the international summer students at Trinity College told us to stay away from the north. *Nothing to see there.* It was 1991, years before the peace process started, and I can't say they were wrong to want to protect us from, for instance, getting caught up in a bombing at a pub. Or even to spare us the kinds of questions posed in one of the Belfast writer Ciaran Carson's best-known poems, "Belfast Confetti": *What is/My name? Where am I coming from? Where am I going? A fusillade of question marks.*

That brief, long-ago visit to Belfast was not the welcome kind of disorientation I found in Frankfurt; it was tense and disturbing. I was wary of the city, I had a less sophisticated understanding of the political and cultural contexts than I thought, and Belfast seemed equally wary of me—a twenty-year-old woman with a tatty backpack and too much curiosity. One pub had been recommended to me by an acquaintance in Dublin: when I entered, I got the stranger in a Western movie saloon treatment—as soon as I stepped over its threshold, conversation halted and all eyes were on me.

No one in pub asked me my name, or where I was from, or where I was going, but I felt the tension hanging in the smoky barroom air. And I couldn't get back to Dublin soon enough.

The tug of my old friendships in Dublin made me want to return to Ireland as often as I could, but like most American visitors, I think it is fair to say, I had no interest in going up north. I had unhappy memories of the place, and could think of no good reason to revisit it.

That changed in 2010, when a friend who edited and wrote travel books returned from a visit to Belfast brimming with excitement about the city. She raved about the beautiful, new hotel she stayed in, whose cocktail bar had quickly become legend among international drinkers. She praised the pubs. And, most persuasively, she spoke of the spirit of the city and its people—of warmth and humor and openness, and an enthusiasm for visitors which had had little outlet during three decades of deadly conflict. If I hadn't been to Belfast lately, she said, *go*.

Her unqualified recommendation was one good reason to give Belfast, and Northern Ireland, another chance, but I had another. At a conference in Louisville, Kentucky, in the early 2000s, Frank had chaired a panel on contemporary Irish literature, and I joined him on the trip. Louisville appealed to me for many reasons: among them, Muhammad Ali, Thomas Merton, Hadley pottery, fried chicken, and bourbon. Frank's Irish literature panel interested me, too. One of the presenters gave a great talk on the poetry of Ciaran Carson. Before the conference, Frank and I had known nothing about him. After the talk, we resolved to read everything Carson had ever published, a prolific, genre-crossing body of work that includes poetry, translation, fiction, and nonfiction.

There were many contemporary Irish writers I already loved, but Carson jumped to the top of the list. And nearly a decade later, I arranged a trip to Belfast so I could meet him, a writer who seldom read publicly, who didn't travel to the U.S. often, who wasn't especially interested in the book tour circuit. I pitched a profile of him to a poetry website I'd written for before, and the editor said yes. Carson's email address was easy to find via the website of Queen's University Belfast, where he was the director of the Seamus Heaney Centre. He agreed to the interview, and we set a date.

Had it not been for Frank, I wondered, would I even have learned about Carson? Maybe—I read poetry almost every day, and sometimes it feels like the only constant in an otherwise messy life. But maybe not. And as nervously excited as I was to meet him, it felt unfair that Frank hadn't had the chance.

I arrived in Belfast on a gray October evening, to a still and quiet city, and checked into the hotel where my friend had stayed. I'd picked up a bad cold at the book fair—the "Frankfurt flu," some called it—and my head was heavy and my throat sore. When I unzipped my suitcase, I rooted around for the microcassette recorder I'd packed for my interview with Carson. It had taken a beating in transit and was so warped that I couldn't even open it. I asked the concierge if the hotel had a recorder available I might borrow. It did not—and the concierge made it clear that Belfast wasn't the sort of place where I'd be able to buy a new one on a Sunday, especially with night closing in. I'd manage: I'd brought plenty of notepads.

I took a walk around the neighborhood and looked into the windows of the local pubs, deciding which ones I'd visit. I walked down the brightly lighted, cobbled street where the Duke of York—a pub I'd read about, where a teenaged Gerry Adams pulled pints and was described by one customer as "a pleasant enough young barman"—was located, and where its patrons sat and smoked and drank on bright red benches outside. I was getting a good feeling from Belfast this time around. I returned to my hotel, freshened up, and went to the cocktail bar.

I ordered a martini, and it was a good one: ice cold and bright, not too dry, festooned with a vibrant curl of lemon peel. The young barman and I chatted—he was friendly, in that gracious, not-*too*-friendly hotel-bar way. By the time my second drink landed in front of me, three women in their mid-fifties sat down on the barstools beside mine. They were old friends on a weekend holiday, up from Dublin to see, like me, what Belfast was all about, and they were having a fabulous time.

Had I been to Ireland before? one of them asked me. Did I like it? What was it like, being a woman traveling on my own? Was it not more fun to travel with a friend, a partner, *my husband?*

I told them I liked traveling alone, which was true: I prefer not to be at the mercy of anyone's schedule but my own, which is usually loose. Frank and I had very different traveling styles. I'm happy to visit a museum or two, then park myself in a pub or café and strike up conversation with strangers. Frank was always determined to pack as much as possible into every trip. Once, when we were in London together, we spent the morning at the British Museum and the National Portrait Gallery. We crossed the Thames under a hostile sun and walked to the Tate Modern. There, in its vast turbine-hall lobby, among enormous, blood-red sculptures, I melted down like an overstimulated four-year-old. I would not walk another step. I could not look at one more portrait, one more statue, one more study for a painting. I sat on a bench and told Frank to enjoy the museum without me, and to take his time, I'd stay right here. Back then, we had no idea and no reason to think that Frank's life would be so short. Now, it seemed poignant to me that Frank wanted to see and do so much every day—and possible that my more leisurely (or maybe just lazy) way of doing things had been wrong. Maybe I had missed out.

I told the women at the bar everything: about Frank, his death, the cancer that killed him, the cat at the funeral parlor, the "mystery woman" (Doris! from the funeral home!) who brought gladioli to the memorial service. I told them about the things he loved, the work he did, his favorite books, the particular way he cocked his head when, I knew, he was perplexed or carefully considering something. I told them about our courtship, and our challenges, and the intensity and fear and moments of reprieve during his final two years alive. And, as I had felt with my old friends in Dublin, I felt more at ease talking about Frank's death with these women, these *Irish* women, than I did in New York. They looked me in the eyes when I spoke about him, about cancer, and death, and grief. They lay the full weight of their hands on my shoulders. It was almost as though, at least in the moment, they were grieving with me, and perhaps they were.

"Aw, pet, he was too young. And you're too young, too."

The women huddled around me in a group hug, and when my tears spilled onto one's silk blouse, they hugged tighter. Avatars of kindness, merciful and compassionate, hearts wide open. The Three Graces, I thought. They returned to their barstools, and we ordered one more round. One of the women suggested a toast to Frank. We lifted our glasses. *To Frank. Always in your heart, and always watching over you.* After I finished my third drink, we hugged one more time, and I went back to my room. I fell asleep feeling warm and secure and grateful for the sweetness and care—even love, yes, what I felt was love—shown to me by three strangers.

Up early the next day to get ready for my interview with Ciaran Carson, I reread some of his poems, a portion of his novel *Shamrock Tea*, the beginning of *Last Night's Fun* (his book about Irish traditional music that's also about everything else). I fussed over what to wear—would casual be okay? or something more professional? He was known to be a sharp dresser. We would meet in the cocktail bar at the hotel at 11 a.m.—as pleasant a place to have coffee or tea as a martini or daiquiri. He approved of the venue.

I arrived about ten minutes early, to get a table. He walked in exactly on time, looking like a flawless cinematic vision of a poet-professor, with his horn-rimmed glasses, his hair neatly cropped, his attire as meticulous and elegant as advertised—most notably a perfectly tailored tweed jacket. I knew that I'd missed his birthday by only a few days, and wished him a happy one, belatedly, when we shook hands.

He stroked the lapels of his jacket. "This was my gift to myself."

"I was admiring it when you walked in."

"Straight off the rack from TK Maxx," he said, suddenly looking as much like a mischievous schoolboy as a great Irish poet. (TK Maxx is the European version of America's TJ Maxx). It wasn't how I had expected a conversation with Ciaran Carson to start, and I loved it.

"My tape recorder broke," I told him, "and I couldn't find a replacement."

"Good," he said. "Tape recorders lie."

This wasn't going to be a typical interview. We wouldn't just sit in a hotel lounge talking. Carson was generous with his time, and had a plan in mind: he would give me a tour of the Falls Road area where he grew up and some other city sights, and afterward he would bring me to the Seamus Heaney Centre in South Belfast's university quarter, where we could, in the end, just sit and talk. But first, he had another idea: TK Maxx was just down the street. We finished our tea and coffee, and a few minutes later I was walking the aisles of a discount department store with one of Ireland's greatest living writers, who showed me the exact spot where he'd found the perfect tweed jacket.

Then we got into his car—a small one, as I remember it. He rolled himself the first of many cigarettes he'd smoke during the afternoon—the tidiest and most uniform rollies I'd ever seen, each nearly as skinny as a cocktail straw, which he chain-smoked for the rest of the day. When we got to the Falls, he took me to the site of his boyhood home; the house itself no longer stands. We talked about his family, his books, his teaching career, the Troubles—and why he chose never to live anywhere but Belfast, despite offers in America, England, and Australia. That old thing, he said: "better the Devil you know."

At the Seamus Heaney Centre, he gave me a tour of the modest building and small backyard garden, proud that some students had taken the initiative to grow things there. We smoked one last cigarette together, and he drove me back to the hotel. When I returned to my room, I looked at the scribblings in my notebook. I'd enjoyed Carson's company, and the unexpected arc of our time together, so much that I hadn't written much down.

That night, I decided I'd had enough of hotel-bar cocktails, and what I needed was a pint or two at a cozy pub. I'd clocked the one right across the street from the hotel: small, homey, invitingly cluttered. The head cold I'd arrived in Belfast with hadn't gotten any better.

"A pint of—" I started to croak my order to the barman.

He stopped me mid-sentence and said, "A hot whiskey for you, then."

His authority impressed me, and I didn't argue. He was right: a hot whiskey would do me more good than a pint of stout. There weren't many available barstools, but I found one in the front corner. I loved the scale of the room, the low ceilings to which classic LP covers were pinned, the loosely thematic bits of bric-a-brac and nods to Spain—and the mix of drinkers, old and young, men and women, quietly alone or boisterously grouped.

It was my kind of bar, but there was one problem: it stank. Really, it reeked—as though a stagnant, fetid pond lay just beneath it, into which the bar might be sinking.

The woman to my right turned to me. "You're lucky your drink smells good," she said. It surprised me to find out that she was an off-duty Belfast police constable—I can't say I knew what the type is, but she didn't strike me as the type—out with her friends for a night on the town. Belfast born and bred, she loved her city and was proud of it, even when her work showed her the worst of it almost every day. She was thrilled to see more tourists returning and gave me a list of recommendations. She asked what had brought me to Belfast, and I told her I was a writer, and described to her my dreamlike afternoon with Ciaran Carson in detail.

When the stench was no longer bearable—the bar's drainage system and the city's antique network of sewers were often at odds, I learned—she said, "we have to get out of here. Since you're a writer you should follow us. We're going to the Hewitt—that's where writers drink." The John Hewitt pub was only a few minutes' walk away.

I'd just ordered my first pint when the guy standing next to me struck up a conversation. The first thing he told me was that he was a Catholic and went to mass daily. I doubted this was something anyone would've announced to a stranger in a Belfast pub even just a decade earlier. It seemed like a strange way to start a chat with a stranger, but what mattered, I thought, was that he felt safe declaring it to me, in this bar, in (as far as I could tell) mixed company.

What *was* I? he wanted to know.

And there I was, in a cozy, busy pub that rightly prided itself on its excellent variety of craft beers and real ales from Ireland and England and elsewhere; where young, sweet-faced musicians played traditional airs and reels on a small stage just beside the front door; where a soft fire burned in a small hearth; in a pub, I learned from reading a brochure tucked inconspicuously into a corner, that was owned and operated by a local nonprofit agency, the Belfast Unemployed Resource Centre, which was founded by the bar's namesake, the Belfast poet and socialist John Hewitt (whom I've also heard, in a nice comic irony, was a teetotaler). There I was, in this warm, welcoming place that existed largely to benefit programs and services for unemployed citizens of Belfast, being asked directly: *What was I?* I felt unmenaced by the question, and by its asker, but was surprised. I wondered what it meant, or mattered, to him: my sense was that he was luxuriating in the freedom to declare who and what he was, which I figured he, as my contemporary, hadn't always been able to exercise, and wanted to extend the same freedom to me. But if anyone had asked me that question in 1991, I think I would have panicked.

I could have given him a long, complicated, honest answer: that I was Jewish, that my parents were Jewish, that my family wasn't religious at all, that I more than dabbled in paganism as a teenager, that I had flirted with a strain of radical dissenting seventeenth-century Christianity in college, that in certain moments when the desire to flee hit me hard, I thought that joining the last surviving Shaker colony seemed like an appealing option, that I was ordained as an interfaith minister and was a Red Cross emergency chaplain in the aftermath of 9/11, that, really, interfaith was exactly how I felt, how I lived, a little bit of this, a little bit of that, whatever works. But I kept it simple and said, "I'm Jewish."

He hadn't expected that, but he was open, and curious. We stepped outside for a smoke. It was raining less now but had gotten late, and Donegall Street was dark. I could just make out the figure of a white-haired man in a long woolen overcoat approaching the bar, brandishing a copy of that day's *Belfast Telegraph*. He knew my new drinking buddy, and walked right up to him. "Did you see this?" the older man asked.

It wasn't anything about a bombing, a murder, politics. The news was that, in a poll, *Telegraph* readers had chosen the Undertones' punk anthem "Teenage Kicks" as Northern Ireland's favorite song.

"It's one of my favorites, too," I said.

The man glowered at me. "Oh, you know it?"

I rolled my eyes. "John Peel's favorite."

"Oh, you know who John Peel was?" He sounded doubtful.

Did any punk rock, indie music lover of my generation not

know who John Peel was? It had probably been Frank who'd told me about him: the great British DJ, a champion of many of the best bands of my youth, and before, and after. I'd encountered this kind of condescension before, in Ireland and elsewhere in Europe: an instant assumption that Americans know nothing. The older guy and I had a quick, terse argument, and by the time he'd stepped inside the bar, I'd written him off as a prick.

My smoking companion told me that the man's name was Terri Hooley, that he was known as the godfather of Northern Irish punk rock, that he ran an indie record store in the city, and that it was he, in fact, who had delivered the demo of "Teenage Kicks" to John Peel. I was impressed. But I still didn't like him. I returned to the bar, and to my drink, and finished up. I said goodnight to the constable and her friends, and in a tiny notebook I'd bought in Dublin, and which I wish I hadn't lost some time later, the constable wrote a short, rhymed poem—the gist of which was: thank you for coming to Belfast, for being open to it, and come back soon.

The next day, as I walked around the city, I happened upon Terri Hooley's record shop, Good Vibrations. The shop clerk, a young man in a rockabilly getup, with a dark, slick crest of pompadour, asked if I was looking for something in particular. I thanked him, and said I was just having a browse. Clocking my accent, he couldn't help but tease me—take the piss, as they say here and elsewhere in Ireland and the United Kingdom, and it was dawning on me that the piss-takers of Belfast might just be the pastime's world champions.

"You've come all the way to Belfast to visit a record shop?" he asked.

"No." I shook my head. "But since it's here, why not?"

"Stick around for a few more minutes. The boss is on his way back. You might like to meet him." He picked a copy of Hooley's then-new memoir, *Hooleygan*, off the front counter. I told him that I'd met the boss last night, that it had not gone well, and I really must be going. Before I could escape, Terri sauntered into the shop, like he owned the place (which he did).

He glowered at me again and said, "Last night at the Hewitt."

I glowered back. And I don't remember how it happened, what had changed, how we softened, but within an hour, hostility had shifted into fondness. We talked about music, joked about New York and Belfast, and, before we said goodbye, we hugged. I bought a copy of *Hooleygan*, and he inscribed his name and drew a flower for me on the title page.

The next day on Facebook, he proposed—or it seemed like a proposal, anyway. He called me "the future Mrs. Hooley." Later, I'd learn that Terri calls almost every woman he meets "the future Mrs. Hooley"—a running joke in Belfast, at least among those who know him, and everyone in Belfast seems to know him. But he also wrote something that touched me more than even a (real) proposal would have: "Belfast needs you."

Although it was just flattery, I teared up. I hadn't felt needed in a long time, since Frank died. Instead, I had felt very needy. And whether Belfast needed me or not (and I was certain it would do just fine without me), it felt possible that I needed Belfast, where friendships can begin as skirmishes outside bars.

That night, I returned to the small, dark pub across from my hotel, where the bartender had so wisely served me that hot whiskey (I could've used another—my cold hadn't gotten any better).

The stench that had driven me out on that earlier occasion was gone, and there was an empty stool at the front corner of the bar—in any bar, the corner's my favorite spot. It was a quieter night: there was an empty barstool beside mine. A man with dark, longish hair and bright blue eyes sat down and ordered a pint. He glanced over at me, a quick look that said *I haven't seen you here before*, bantered with the bartender—this time, a young woman, who also made an excellent hot whiskey.

He was funny, and quick-witted and fast-talking, another cheerful, skillful Belfast piss-taker. I picked up cues that said I was welcome to join in the conversation, so I did. The bartender went back to mixing drinks and pulling pints, and he and I kept talking. His name was Mark, he worked at one of the restaurants in my hotel, and he was also a sculptor. He ordered us another round and asked what I was doing in Belfast, and where I was from. "New York," I told him. "Brooklyn."

"I usually don't like Americans," he said. "But you're alright."

Here we go again, I thought, and told him I'd long since tired of kneejerk anti-American attitudes like his, that they were unimaginative, dull, and just not very smart. But I liked him anyway—he was curious, interested in my work and my experience of Belfast, and everywhere else I'd been in my travels. He ordered us another round. We talked and laughed and argued some more. But I was leaving the next day, and still not feeling well, so it couldn't be a late night out. Our next and final round was on me.

"A pleasure," I said, as I got up to leave. "Even if you don't like Americans."

"If you're ever back in Belfast, let me know," he said. By then, I was sure I would be back in Belfast, as soon as possible. Sure, I'd look him up next time. But what I didn't know yet was how close we would become. Sometimes even the most real friendships start in pubs—with an insult.

I didn't feel ready to go home, and was less certain than ever about what "home" meant. When I boarded the plane, I felt both physically sick and sick at heart. To return to New York meant a return, I believed, to the stasis of the grief I'd left there.

That didn't mean that grief had abandoned me while I was away, but it had transformed. I often thought of Frank when I was away—in Germany and London, where we had traveled together. But I also thought of him many times in Belfast. When I made it clear to Terri Hooley that, yes, I knew "Teenage Kicks," and I knew who John Peel was, the truth was that, had it not been for Frank, I probably wouldn't have. It was Frank who had opened my mind so much wider than it had been when we met, who not only joyfully shared his passions with me, but also advocated for them—gently, but persuasively. *You like the Pogues? You should give the Undertones and Stiff Little Fingers a chance, too.*

For the first time since he had died, but not the last, I felt that, somehow, I was, if not quite living his life for him, having experiences that he should have had instead. It is a kind of magical thinking to which the loss of a loved one extends itself—while the loved one is somewhere, nowhere, dead, not alive, *in absentia*, his survivor becomes his proxy, understudy, and, sometimes, maybe, usurper.

Sometimes, I felt like he would have been proud—if not of me, of the depth of his influence. But other times, maybe most of the time, I felt guilty. Had I not accompanied Frank to that academic conference in Louisville, would I have even known about Ciaran Carson? And had I not known about Ciaran Carson, would I have bothered to make that trip to Belfast?

Frank should have been in that record shop, listening to Terri's wild stories about its early days, talking about the bands that came through Belfast during the Troubles, about how punk rock brought Belfast kids together across the sectarian divide and over its physical and psychological walls. It should have been Frank who heard about how the music and the energy and the sense of fellowship defined by something other than religion probably saved some young lives. I knew that one line in the song his friends sang at the funeral reception—Minutemen's "History Lesson—Part II"—was most meaningful to him: *Punk rock changed our lives.* I sometimes thought that Frank—who had not grown up in a war zone like his Belfast contemporaries, but grew up bookish and shy, dislocated and misunderstood and often unhappy in a distant suburb of San Francisco—felt that punk rock had changed his life, too—even saved it.

Back in Brooklyn, I lay sick in bed for another week. I kept thinking about Belfast, trying to plot out how and when I might go back. There were other cities I loved, including the one I lived in, where I was born, where I had spent almost my entire life. But Belfast excited me because it looked and felt like a city that was getting better, opening up, coming back to itself, to vibrant life, after a long, troubled sleep. I couldn't say that New York or London or Dublin—where the cost of rent had become almost impossible for those of us who aren't loaded and where, despite their pleasures and opportunities, everyday life sometimes seemed like a constant battle—were getting better. Belfast felt livable, affordable and, above all, hopeful.

I glanced at the notes I'd taken during my day with Ciaran Carson; they were not only scant, they were also almost illegible: my own handwriting, which is lousy under normal circumstances, had been warped and distended by the antihistamine fog I'd been under. I'd have to follow up with him by email—and the thought of taking up more of his time made me feel even sicker.

A return to Belfast felt inevitable—but it would have to wait. By the time I was back in Brooklyn, my mother, who had been dying for so long, was now near the end. She had had multiple heart attacks. She could no longer eat solid food. She was in pain. From early November until her death at the end of February, I visited her almost every day. The skin on her hands had gone thin as parchment; her body so frail she couldn't hold her head up. She had joked for decades that she wanted her gravestone to say: *Thin at last.* Now that she weighed so little, it wasn't funny anymore.

Her final night in the hospital, her final night, I held her hand as long as the doctors and nurses would let me. *I love you, Ma. I love you.* We had been hard on each other. We had gone through long stretches of estrangement. She loved me. I loved her—and, in the end, that was all that I needed her to know. If love is the thing we all want most and need most, my mother wanted and needed love more than anyone I've ever known.

I never wrote the Ciaran Carson profile. My assigning editor left the poetry website. I couldn't read my own notes—and was so embarrassed about it that I would not email him to explain. I remembered what Carson had said about tape recorders: they lie. Maybe notes did, too, I thought, and tried to build a story from memories of that afternoon. I couldn't do it. After many weeks, I sent him a postcard. I thanked him for his time. I said I would keep him posted on publication. I told him that my mother died. I probably sounded insane—which is how I was feeling. I hoped that I would see him again someday, and do a better job of explaining.

3

ROGER CASEMENT, THE HANDSOME, HORNY DEVIL:
British diplomat, Irish revolutionary, foundational figure in the
history of human rights. Champion of the abused, the maimed,
the enslaved, the exploited—and, arguably, sometimes exploiter
of those whom he championed. At the bottom of his long list of
achievements, far below bearing witness to, and reporting on, human rights atrocities in the Congo and the plight of the people
of the Putumayo, I can add a very minor one: it was he, Roger
Casement—or the ghost of him—who led me to the village of
Glenarm.

In early March 2016, Ireland was calling to me. After another
terrible February, during which my beloved uncle Bill—my father's radical and gracious brother, an idol to me since childhood—
and my nineteen-year-old cat, a constant and loving companion
through the worst of times, both died, I felt flattened by loss again.
It had been five years then since my mother's death, and six years
since Frank's, and even with the passing of so much time, I knew
that my grieving for them was not over yet, nowhere near it.

But in those long years, some extraordinary things, things I never imagined possible, had happened. A friend was asked if she was interested in writing a monthly column called "Drink" for the *New York Times Magazine*. She didn't think it was right for her—and recommended me for the job instead. "I hope you don't mind," she said, when she called to let me know. *Did I mind?* I was awed by her generosity—an angel!—and, even more, by her faith in me; I had little in myself.

When the magazine's editor emailed me to ask if I was interested, I said yes, of course I said *yes*, but I was terrified. The job sounded too good to be true—I didn't even know there was such a job as "drink writer." And the main thing was: Who the hell was *I*? It was impossible that I would get it, I was sure of that, but I was determined at least not to embarrass the friend who'd put me up for it. That summer amounted to a very long audition process— the closest I've ever felt to what I imagine it must be like to be on one of those reality contest shows, in which contestants are given one challenge, then another, and then another. Why not? It was the *Times*—and I was a part-time bartender whose only published writing credit on the subject of drink to date was an essay about W. H. Auden and martinis for a poetry website. Could I write a sample Q&A and send it in by 3 p.m., today? *Okay.* Could I compress that essay into a front-of-book list—by lunch? *If you insist.* Could I send five ideas for possible columns? *Here's ten.* Whenever my email inbox pinged, or my phone rang, I jumped. I did everything I was asked to do, and then a little bit more. And it still seemed like the longest of long shots.

That October, the editor called me in for a meeting, during which he told me I'd made the shortlist. I was given more tasks. I was called in for another meeting. And then, I awoke one morning to an email that said the job was mine.

My brother took me to the Oyster Bar in Grand Central Station that evening to celebrate. After a few sips from a martini, I told him that, as thrilled as I was, there was something about it that also made me sad.

"I wish mom was here to see this."

My brother laughed. He'd thought the same thing. "I know exactly what she would've said: 'Look at *you*, working for a little cable TV sports channel. And look at your sister, working for the *New York Times*.'" He was right. She always had a knack for lifting us up—and then smacking us down. And she'd never appreciated what a great job he had, and how good he is at it, and she had never grasped the popularity of the channel he worked for, the scope of its audience. But *New York Times*? She knew the *New York Times*. The details—that my very cool gig was also very part-time, with no benefits, and no way to predict how long it might last—would not have troubled her.

I was still tending bar when the column launched (and I continued to for many years after). I was also writing my first book. And suddenly, I had a career as a journalist—a thing I'd never planned, and had even, as the daughter of a journalist father, resisted. It was a life that looked to others like nonstop fun: all drinking cocktails and eating delicious food and traveling to beautiful places—and getting paid to write about it. I resolved to charge ahead as a writer and as what some called a "professional drinker," and to push the very unsettled business of my grief aside. Or at least I tried to make it look that way.

I posted cheerfully captioned photos of the cocktails I made (and drank), the columns and other articles I published, the bar and restaurant openings I now found myself wanted at, invited to by people whom I was certain would have looked right past me before I held this strange and influential office.

Meanwhile, contrary to appearances, I was wracked by anxiety, almost broke, in flagging physical and emotional health, and so haunted by Frank's death, and by my absence during the final hours of his life, that I had not only resigned myself to a lonely, loveless future, but had come to believe that I deserved exactly that. Even the very particular kind of good fortune that had found me had an uncanny quality to which Frank was intimately bound.

Before I met Frank, I was hardly what anyone would have called discerning about spirits and cocktails, beer and wine. I loved bars—especially the people and the banter, the community that bars brought together—deeply. I drank beer and cheap wine and Irish whiskey—sometimes gin and tonics on warm summer evenings. An occasional whiskey sour (my mother's drink of choice) or martini (it made me feel like a proper grown-up) was about as far as I went with mixed drinks. But by the time we met in our mid-twenties, Frank already had a signature cocktail, the Manhattan, which he ordered with easy, suave authority. And although I thought I was pretty sophisticated about food, he was, by a very great measure, my superior as a cook, in range, in skill, and in taste. Most of what I know now about cooking and eating well, I learned from him. He'd spent part of his boyhood in Australia, and part in the Netherlands, and had seen much more of the world than I had. Who did I think I was, writing about drink and food and travel? Frank was the expert, not me. And, unlike me, he was a devoted reader of food-and-drink journalism. He and his best friend from high school wrote a cookbook together. He was his college newspaper's restaurant critic. Not long after we married, I signed him up for a food-writing course as a birthday gift, and he loved it—but never pitched the stories he reported and wrote.

There were warm moments when I imagined that perhaps Frank had somehow, in his afterlife, engineered this for me, had rehung the stars in such a way that I might get to do the work which he himself wanted to do, and which he would have loved. That I might get to continue on a path upon which he had only just begun, that he would guide me on my way because Frank was kind, because he believed in me more than anyone ever had, and because he was at peace.

But there were swells of coldness, too, when I felt that Frank had arranged this somehow, in his afterlife, to tell me: *You can have this, but it won't make you happy. Nothing will. Because you broke my heart. Because you were not there when I died.* Because Frank was angry with me, and resentful, and unquiet in his grave, and why shouldn't he be?

I had warm thoughts, and cold ones. And both made me feel like I was going mad.

In 2016, when Ireland was calling to me again, I stayed up late with my laptop hot on my thighs in my drafty Brooklyn bedroom. To soothe myself enough to fall asleep, I pored over images of grandmotherly cottages and stoic, one-eyed lighthouses, and seaside shacks with salty, weathered faces. There were pretty, cozy houses to be had in Cork and Donegal, in Waterford and Sligo, in Leitrim and Down, Wicklow and Clare, and I could *almost* picture myself in any of them.

Almost—because I had a history of hating holiday houses. They might look pretty on the outside, but I knew what might lurk within: must and mildew and strange smells, and a dispiriting, all-encompassing sense of secondariness, never-quite-lived-in or loved-well-enough-ness. A stained armchair here; a joyless metal stick of floor lamp there; a single, strafed nonstick frying pan in a sticky kitchen cupboard; a bruised black-leather couch inherited from someone's uncle's office renovation.

Or—maybe worse—they could be overdone and bloated: repositories for bric-a-brac no one wants to look at in their *real* home and mementos to which no meaningful memories are attached, catchment areas for the cast-off and the set-aside. Like the house where Frank and I briefly stayed in 2002, during the part of our honeymoon we spent in Scotland's Outer Hebrides, on the Isle of Skye.

On the outside, it was perfect: a simple, stone croft house. But no one warned us about the collection of dead-eyed dolls in tiny ball gowns in the den, the fusty yellowed curtains of nylon ruffles in the dining area, the stinking dust-trap pots of potpourri on every end table. A retired couple owned and oversaw the house. On the surface, they were all smiles and solicitousness, but it was plain as day that they despised each other. We could feel it, and we could see it, and it was not a vision of late married life we newly-weds wanted to know, especially on our honeymoon.

Every hour or so, from the time we arrived, just after lunch, until dusk, they'd knock on our door—the wife or the husband or both—to ask: Did we want a recommendation for a pub? Would we like breakfast in the morning? A hot water bottle before bed? Did we need directions to the, what was it?—the *serpentarium*—down the road?

Were we alright?

No, we are not alright, because we think you might come back in the middle of the night and murder us in our sleep, I thought but did not say, and Frank had thought the same. We lasted one night and checked into a hotel the next day.

With only one exception—a cottage we shared with friends in the English Lake District (another stop on our honeymoon itinerary) a few years after we married, and a few years before Frank got sick—there would be no more holiday houses for us. After Frank was gone, there would be no more for me. I had come to prefer the anonymity and predictability of ordinary budget hotels. My travels were always connected to work, which meant that if I was doing my job, I wouldn't be spending much time inside a hotel room, anyway. I'd be out—seeing, talking, eating, drinking, meeting and interviewing people.

But as I scrolled through those pictures of places where I might stay the next time I went to Ireland, I kept returning to the website of the Irish Landmark Trust, a nonprofit organization that refurbishes derelict historic properties in the north and the south, and lets them out to vacationers. Inside, they were all bright and uncluttered—no dolls, no potpourri. And one in particular pushed its way into my daydreams: a modest, gray gatehouse deep in the County Antrim countryside, close to the town of Ballycastle, with distant views of the North Atlantic. It had two bedrooms. A stone patio. A fireplace. A large, well-equipped country kitchen. A little study tucked into the eaves upstairs.

Neither the most beautiful nor the most luxurious house on the website, it had the most seductive history: it sat at the threshold of Magherintemple, the family estate on which Roger Casement had spent a formative part of his youth, after his parents both died and he was sent to live there with an uncle. Casement: name-checked by Joyce in the "Cyclops" section of *Ulysses* ("Did you read that report by a man what's this his name is? —Casement, says the citizen. He's an Irishman."), memorialized by Yeats in his poem "The Ghost of Roger Casement" ("The ghost of Roger Casement/is beating at the door"). Ever since I'd read those texts as an undergraduate, I was interested in him.

Casement had been knighted for his humanitarian work in the Amazon. But the atrocities he witnessed there, and in Africa, altered his perspective on the British Empire. Later, as a committed Irish revolutionary, he was involved in a scheme to secure support and arms from Germany; it did not go well. On his return from Germany on Good Friday, 1916, he was captured in County Kerry. He was charged with treason.

Casement was also, to his detriment, an indefatigable documentarian of his daily life: the explicit accounts in his diary of sex with men, though not presented in court at his trial, turned some who had been sympathetic against him, and thwarted any chance of clemency. He was executed by hanging on August 3, 1916, at London's Pentonville Prison.

Roger Casement: long gone, long dead, but still here, still haunting us, still beating on the door, still with us, if we care, if we answer and let him in.

There could be a story here, I thought that night, as I clicked on that page on the website, over and over. And if I was lucky, that story might pay my way back to Ireland; that was the only way it would be possible.

The next day, a newspaper travel section editor I knew emailed me. "You should write a travel piece sometime!" he said. I slowly reread the email—the timing was so good, I had to make sure I hadn't dreamed it—and wrote back immediately.

Yes, thank you, I would *love* to write for Travel, I told him. In fact, I said, as if in saying so I was making it true, as I had not yet booked the house and wasn't even sure it would be available, I was heading to Ireland in May, where I would be staying on the grounds of the country estate where Roger Casement spent his adolescence.

"I feel like there may be something there," I wrote. "Can human rights tourism be a thing?" Sure it could. The editor gave his blessing, and I booked the gate lodge at Magherintemple for three nights in mid-May.

Meanwhile, a beloved friend was having a tough time.

Katherine, a fellow journalist, had spent much of the previous year shuttling between New York and the small Midwestern city where she had grown up, to visit her parents in the assisted living facility where both were in declining health. It was painful being far away. It was also painful being up close. With no other relatives able to look after them, to make sure that the staff knew there was someone who cared, someone keeping an eye, someone tending to the endless paperwork and making the decisions her mother and father could no longer make for themselves, Katherine was dutiful and loving.

That winter, her mother died, and, only weeks later, her father did, too. And when the first death came, and then the next, she was drained, exhausted, and unmovably sad, in the way, I knew, that only the loss of those we love most makes us.

By early spring, it seemed that she had started to shake off the heaviest weight of grief—but was still stricken by it in unpredictable waves. On the phone one night I mentioned to her that I'd gotten a great assignment—to go to Ireland and follow the trail of Roger Casement there, from outside Dublin, where he was born, to the Antrim countryside up north, where he lived as a teenager and where he wished to be buried, and that the story would be published on the one hundredth anniversary of his execution.

Katherine had never been to Ireland.

I told her about the cottage I'd booked: its history, its two cozy bedrooms, its wood-burning fireplace and flagstone patio. I told her about its big, homey kitchen; we both love to cook, and had often cooked together with easy, relaxed joy—a thing I consider a mark of a true and durable friendship. And I told her how I'd been feeling low and longing for the countryside, the Irish countryside.

"You should come with me," I said. Katherine was grieving; of course she should come to Ireland. Wasn't grief—along with the stunning coastline, the hills and glens, the poetry, the pubs, and the craic—one of the things Ireland did best? She booked her flights.

I asked Mark, the bartender/sculptor I'd met in Belfast in 2010, if he could recommend a driver to take Katherine and me to Magh-

erintemple, and he referred me to his friend Seamus. Mark—
the guy who had told me by way of introduction that he hated
Americans, but won me over anyway—and I had by then become
friends, in touch regularly, mostly by email, at least some of which
he'd written and sent after a few pints, and which always made me
laugh. We met up whenever I was in Belfast. On one of those occasions he'd surprised me by taking me on a date. It had taken some
time for me to catch on that that's what it was. We'd met up at the
same bar as usual, then went to dinner. He insisted on picking up
the tab—but that's not a sure sign of a date. He suggested another
pub for an after-dinner drink, and we walked there, through a city
I still didn't know well, through a shopping mall, and then into
an alley, where he kissed me, and kissed me again, and I liked his
kisses. The romance grew with almost every further visit, but I still
thought of us as friends—how could we be more than that, living
on opposite sides of the Atlantic Ocean?

Before heading to Magherintemple, Katherine and I spent two
nights in Dublin and two in Belfast. In the former, she came down
with a cold, and in the latter she spent most of her time conva-
lescing in our hotel room. I worried about her. She was sniffly and
groggy when we piled into Seamus's car. I suggested that she sit
up front, the better to take in the views. I'd seen plenty of Irish
countryside before, even if this patch was new to me.

"Will I take the scenic route?" Seamus asked.

"Yes, please!" I said.

"Just promise me there will be sheep," Katherine said sleepily.

"There will be sheep," I promised.

Sheep made their first appearance only minutes after we'd left the
city, in the rolling hills of County Antrim, and tracked alongside us

until we exited onto the Coast Road that curves along the north channel of the Irish Sea. Seamus first took us into Ballycastle, to stock up on groceries and wine. From there, it was just a few minutes' drive to the house. I phoned the property manager and she met us at the gate. Before we opened the door, I asked her if she knew if members of the Casement family still lived in the area. I'd assumed I'd have to do some old-fashioned legwork for my story, and figured I might as well start right away.

She looked puzzled by my question, and pointed her chin toward the big house just up the drive. "Right there," she said. "Patrick Casement. If you want to meet him, go and ask him if you can buy some firewood." Could it be as easy as that?

After we'd settled into the gate lodge, Katherine and I walked up to the big house to ask for firewood. No one was home, so we left a note on the back door. An hour later, Patrick Casement approached with a wheelbarrow full of logs. He asked if I'd like to see the house—and Katherine, with her usual grace, suggested that I go with Patrick and she stay back and prep for dinner. Her journalist instincts knew that some time on my own with him, in the house where Roger Casement once had lived, would be good for my story.

In the parlor, Patrick showed me a credenza Roger Casement had shipped home from the Amazon, while we discussed his famous, and infamous, relative. And he mentioned he'd recently gone to Kerry, to attend a service commemorating Roger's landing and capture there—and to see an excellent exhibition at the county museum about his brief, but pivotal, time in Kerry. I regretted that I hadn't known about it sooner, that it wasn't on my itinerary.

My story was coming together faster than I'd expected. And that gatehouse! How Katherine and I loved it, and our meadow, and the woods, full of birdsong, against which the house nestled, and our complement of fat, content sheep. And our little patio—where we drank rosé and ate sardines on buttered toast and packets of prawn cocktail crisps at sunset. And the weather: it seemed impossible, four days of blazing sunshine in Ireland? In *Northern Ireland*? On each of the three mornings we awakened at Magherintemple, we made our coffee, stepped outside with our mugs, looked around, and laughed, just because it was so beautiful, and because we felt so lucky to be there. It is one thing, and not a bad thing, to remind oneself to be grateful. It is another to feel gratitude overtake oneself completely, without effort or will.

We hadn't even noticed, until our last day, that Katherine's miserable cold had disappeared almost on arrival at Magherintemple. Years later, we both still look back on our too-brief time there as one of complete contentment, and, in a small, sweet way, of healing.

My friend Rosita lives in Dublin, but she is a daughter of the Irish West, born and raised in County Clare. She'd hitchhiked all of Ireland's coastline in her twenties—and, with the Troubles still raging then, she felt little love for the North. But when I told her about the Casement story, and the gatehouse on his family's estate, she—also a writer—was curious. Might she drive up and stay with us for a night?

She pulled up in her little white car at the golden hour, when saturated pre-sunset light filtered through the foliage, lighting the edges of the cottage, making a dreamy, gilded mural of the whole scene—I thought of Maxfield Parrish. Katherine and I had poured the evening's first aperitifs on the patio, and we couldn't have been more thrilled by the house, the light, the sweet air, our good fortune, ourselves.

I made Rosita a drink as she strode toward us, her red curls fiery in the evening sun. She scrutinized our trees, our meadow, our sheep, our setting sun. She was judging our splendid little cottage.

"Well, it's *pretty*," she said, casting her eyes around. "But it's not the West, is it?"

Not even that could break the spell Magherintemple had cast on Katherine and me—not that I thought that's what Rosita had meant to do. I had gleaned, over many years and many visits, some idea of what Irish people from one part of the island think of its other parts. During a raucous dinner with friends in Dublin years earlier, my dining companions burst into a fit of laughter when they read on the menu that the free-range chicken had been sourced from a farm in County Cavan. "They must be very mean chickens," one said. By "mean" she meant stingy, miserly—not unkind, the way we mean it in the States. That, and didn't I know that the people of Cavan always sound like they're whining? Then they treated me to a catalog of regional stereotypes, county by county. People from Meath—"the royal county"—are snobs. People from Cork are hopeless homers, convinced that their county is the center of the universe and sure why would anyone ever leave? People from Kerry: mad as a box of frogs.

And there's the line I've heard about the North, in many variations: no matter what someone from Northern Ireland says, it sounds like they're making a threat. Even if they're just asking for a cup of tea or the time of day.

There is some evidence that people from the Irish West—its sixteen-hundred-mile coastline, stretching from Cork to Donegal, was successfully branded by Irish Tourism "the Wild Atlantic Way"—regard their portion of the island as the most authentic, most Irish Ireland, the genuine article, the real thing. Every time this notion of the Irish West is expressed to me, I think of Miss Ivors, in Joyce's story "The Dead," an opinionated nationalist who tries to shame the protagonist, Gabriel Conroy, into forgoing another holiday on the continent in favor of a trip to the Aran Islands, about as far west as one can go in Ireland. "And haven't you your own land to visit," she asks him, "that you know nothing of, your own people, and your own country?" Ivors's implication is clear: it is the West where one can best know Ireland. If he can be said to belong to any West, he is, she says, a "West Briton." It stings him.

I want to tread lightly with all stereotypes (ones that flatter, and ones that do not) about this island and the people who live on it—not only because I am not from there, and not only because I come from a place, New York City, that is also burdened with stereotypes (good and bad, true and, in my own experience, false), but also because, even if they can sometimes be instructive, even if some, maybe many, are rooted in truth, they also strip away texture, dimensionality, vitality, and, perhaps, even greater truths.

That night, after dinner, we brought our drinks into the living room, and Rosita offered to make a fire. "This," she said, as she knelt by the hearth, choosing logs from the pile Patrick Casement delivered to us, "is a rich man's firewood." Here, finally, was one thing up north that impressed her.

In the morning, Rosita had to make an early start. She gave us a lift to Ballycastle harbor, where we would catch the early ferry to Rathlin Island—the northernmost inhabited place in Ireland, known for its rugged beauty, its bloody history (in 1575, more than six hundred islanders were killed in the Rathlin Island Massacre), and its population of puffins, guillemots, kittiwakes, fulmars, and razorbills. I'd read that there was a café on the island, where I expected we would start our day before setting out for the West Light Seabird Centre. After the thirty-minute crossing—there were few other tourists on the boat, mostly people who commuted to the island to work—we docked and went to the café. A note on the door said it was closed; the chef was pregnant, we learned later, and didn't feel up to cooking that day.

A man we'd chatted with on the ferry saw us standing, forlorn, outside the closed café. David was Rathlin Island's lone social worker, and he invited us to his office for a cup of tea and biscuits, apologizing that he didn't have more to offer us.

On the short walk there, Katherine and I had our first puffin sighting: a proud, plump bird parked in the front yard of a cottage, as though keeping guard. We oohed and aahed and all but genuflected at the mild, still creature, and at another instance of the good fortune our time on the Antrim Coast had given us. David, our kind new friend, stood by quietly. He had chosen not to crush us with the truth. Many hours later, after a long hike and a visit to the seabird center, on our way back to the ferry, we were amazed to see the same bird in the same position in the same front yard, and it was only then that we realized we'd been duped by a statue. We returned to Magherintemple tired, sunburned, embarrassed, and deliriously happy. We had one more night there, and already the prospect of having to leave didn't seem fair.

Back in New York, I thought about the exhibition in Kerry that Patrick Casement had told me about. I should have known sooner, and I should have gone. For the sake of my story, and to satisfy my own tendencies, I wanted to be a Casement completist. But mostly I thought about the Antrim countryside, and wished I was still there, wished I hadn't left. There was one other important local site on the Casement trail I'd skipped: Murlough Bay, at the outermost northeastern edge of Ireland, a place Casement loved, the place where he wished to be buried. I should have gone there, too.

So I did something I'd never done before: I asked my editor if there was any chance of increasing my expenses budget. It seemed unlikely, but I gave it a shot, and explained to him that visiting a few more sites would round out reporting and make for a better story. He said yes. It wouldn't be much, but if I found a cheap flight, I could make it work. I might not make any money from this Casement adventure, but I'd break even, and that was good enough for me, if not for my debtors.

Patrick Casement was right about the exhibition: it was beautifully curated, informative, and moving. The sight of the small dinghy in which he hit the shores of Banna Strand made me feel his presence in a way I hadn't elsewhere during my reporting. The museum's curator took me to other Casement sites in the area, including the beach where he landed.

After a few days in County Kerry, I made my way back to

County Antrim on buses and trains. I hired Seamus, who'd driven Katherine and me to Magherintemple, to take me up to remote, windswept Murlough Bay, and Mark joined us for the journey. A simple wooden cross stands there, and a small stone memorial to Casement. It was easy to see why he loved it there, and why he would have chosen it as his final resting place. Murlough Bay was not only the most beautiful and serene place I'd seen on the whole of the Irish island, but one of the most beautiful places I'd visited anywhere, ever. And I felt his presence even more powerfully than I had at the exhibition in Kerry.

History is a powerful magnet, pulling us toward places we have read about or heard about or studied closely, places associated with people we admire (or revile), places where we know *something happened*—even if it is not "our" history, even if they are not, by birth or by heritage, "our" places, although when they are, the pull may be even more powerful. To visit a site because of its history cannot be an act of witness, because history is past. But it is an act of memorialization: a spoken or unspoken "here lived." To visit historic sites can also be a kind of magical thinking, even magical action, much like visiting a loved one's grave: if I bring myself to this place, I will forge or deepen my connection to this place, and to the people who once lived here. And I will try not to consider the obvious—that the dead can have no knowledge of our intentions—because, then, the spell will break.

Well aware of my bad habits, I knew that if I didn't write a draft of the story immediately after I wrapped up my reporting, and before returning to Brooklyn, I'd succumb to distractions and procrastinate until the last minute. So I booked three nights at another Irish Landmark Trust property that had captured my attention when I saw it online: the Barbican, the fairy-tale castle folly at the entrance to Glenarm Castle. The village had all I'd need for a short stay: a grocery store and two pubs just down the street, a forest and coastline for head-clearing walks. The village seemed perfect.

That remained true even when I came down with norovirus after my first night in Glenarm. Mark came up from Belfast. He brought me ginger ale and crackers, the only food I thought I could stomach. He also made me soup—in case I changed my mind. He'd never seen me ill before, and I'd never seen him like this: a gentle and attentive caregiver. And that's when I thought, he might be more than a friend. I saw yet another side of Mark that was new to me: the nature lover, the walker in the woods, the man who dreamily remembered easy, happy boyhood days spent fishing with his grandfather, the student who had majored in ecology. Glenarm is small enough that he had never heard of it, and he fell under its spell as fast as I had—enchanted by the seashore, the forest, the light, the quiet.

But Glenarm had more than that. It had a feeling, a spirit, a strong sense of place to which I succumbed. I knew I would be back. And I had a feeling that someday I would stay much longer. The ghost of Roger Casement had beaten at my door. I answered, and, in some way, he led me home.

4

AFTER MY SUMMER IN DUBLIN IN 1991, I HAD AL-
ways wanted to live in Ireland again—someday. But Brooklyn? I
never wanted to live there. Brooklyn was where my parents came
from, and, for all their nostalgia (*Ebbets Field! The Coney Island
Ferris Wheel! Ebinger's Bakery!*) it was the place from which their
own parents had fled with them as quickly as they could. Brooklyn
was not for me. Still, that's where I wound up living in 1996, the
year I met Frank. I was twenty-five.

My favorite college professor lived there and liked it, and she
knew I had to leave the apartment I had shared in lower Manhattan. She also knew there was an apartment open in the building
next door to hers, in an unfamiliar (to me) neighborhood that was
"Park Slope South," or "South Slope," or something. She urged me
to come take a look. There was no harm in that.

To get there, I walked one block uphill from the nearest subway
station, past a row of handsome brick town houses and dignified
brownstones. And there she was, without contest the ugliest house
on the south side of the street: a squat, stunted stump of a building

sheathed in bruised white aluminum siding. I considered turning back.

Behind that siding, however, it was a different story. The vacant second-floor apartment had high ceilings and six tall windows, three of which faced north onto Seventeenth Street and onto the chimneys of the Polish delicatessen around the corner on Fifth Avenue, through which billowed the meaty incense of freshly smoked kielbasy. The other windows faced south onto the pocket gardens and workaday backyards of Eighteenth Street and sunlight soaked through them, light that stirred my vestigial Dutchness, light that felt like lowlands light, de Hooch light, Vermeer light, clean and expansive. But then, this was a borough brimming with Dutchness, at least in its place names: Boerum, Bushwick, Flatbush, Utrecht, Brooklyn itself.

There was a bathroom with a window and a claw-footed, cast-iron tub, black and white tiled floors, a linen closet. What twenty-five-year-old person had her own linen closet? In an alcove beside the kitchen there was a deep pantry. And, next to the bedroom, a narrow chamber that could make a cozy office. If I moved in, I would need more linens. More dishes, more pots and pans. I'd need office things. Adult things.

The rent for the apartment was cheap compared to the rent for places I'd looked at in Manhattan, none of which I could afford, and though it was no more than 450 square feet, it was easily twice their size. When Susan, the friendly, chatty landlady, whisked me into her apartment one flight below to talk money and review the lease, I saw a poster of the New York City Labor Chorus on one of her kitchen walls, and on the opposite an even larger poster of Nelson Mandela, and thought, maybe this place will be alright.

I signed the lease and resolved to suck it up for a year, save some money, then move back to Manhattan, where I was born and raised and rightly belonged.

Unsurprisingly, for all their schmaltzy sentiment about the borough, my parents saw my move to Brooklyn, even if it was temporary, as a sure sign of generational downward mobility. They were not wrong.

I hired an all-woman moving company to shift my small inventory of belongings across the East River: bed, desk, chair, books, an area rug, some pots and pans. The crew comprised a small, strong forewoman and two gangly, punk-rock Dutch girls on an extended holiday lark. "Never leave this place," one of them said as she deposited the last box of books on the bedroom floor with a soft thud. "It has a good feeling." Her colleagues agreed. I did, too. It did have a good feeling. It would be fine. For a year.

Twenty-three years later, I swept the kitchen floor for the last time. I zipped up three duffel bags and two suitcases, lugged them downstairs, handed Susan my keys, and hugged her. Then I stood on the stoop and waited for a taxi to take me away.

Acquisitiveness is an embarrassment to a twenty-five-year-old Marxist, who is supposed to be a Materialist in the big-M, dialectical way, not in the distasteful little-m way, who is not supposed to concern herself with the amassing, collecting, and displaying of stuff. And yet, I couldn't help myself. Give me a room, even one I might occupy only for a single, fleeting Vermont summer, and I will find things to fill it. There is a strain of self-psychologizing I could go into right now—my family moved around a lot! we never really had a home!—but I won't. I think it is more pertinent only to confess that I like things, and I have always liked things, even if this has sometimes created both philosophic and emotional discomfort, seeming as it does to be at odds with other, greater concerns, like social justice and the destruction of the natural world.

When I say I like things, I do not mean expensive, luxurious things, although of course there are some expensive, luxurious things I like very much, just as there are things I have found discarded on sidewalks and things I have rooted around for in curbside trash cans, chancing contact with dog shit and discarded needles, that I love as much, if not more.

I'm talking about things that give me pleasure; things I like to look at and touch and think about; things that do not breathe, that are not living, but which nonetheless make life better and more interesting—which is the job of style, which is why style is a good in itself. Those who disagree, who underestimate style, who dismiss it as unimportant, do so, I assume, because they do not have it.

I will take bad taste over no style any day. Bad taste can bestow its own funny kind of joy. No style is ungenerous: it gives nothing, does nothing, says nothing. Bad taste tells a story, sometimes even a poignant one. No style has only the kind of meaning that is against meaning. It borders on the nihilistic; it is sad.

In decorating my Brooklyn apartment, my role models were my aunt Ellen and uncle Bill, bohemian radicals of the old school, who lived for most of my lifetime in a sprawling warren of rooms right where they belonged, one block west of Washington Square Park, in the heart of Greenwich Village. If they, who had given

shelter to the Black Panthers, who had exposed the activities of
CIA operatives around the world, who had counseled war resist-
ers at home and abroad—if *they* could love beautiful things, and
have beautiful things, surely it was okay for me to love and have
them, too.

Antique Persian carpets covered most of their creaky wooden
floorboards. In the narrow front hall, a gallery of framed portraits
of their heroes lined the yolk-yellow walls. Sacco and Vanzetti.
Emiliano Zapata. John Brown (about whom a friend has aptly
said, "He was crazy. But he was not wrong."). I called their apartment the People's Palace.

Red silk that had aged and softened to persimmon was pinned
to the walls of the living room—but to call it a living room is care-
less. It was a salon, where, save for just a few intrusions of modern
life—a television and cable box, a few framed photographs that
couldn't have been taken before the 1970s—I could easily imagine
Emma Goldman and John Reed arguing the respective merits of
anarchy versus Bolshevism, while draining a bottle of absinthe,
beside the fireplace to which my uncle had painstakingly applied
a faux-finish resembling malachite, under the Victorian tiger's-
eye glass chandelier, the huge Cuban oil painting, the ceremonial
masks from West Africa and Indonesia, and the massive, hand-
painted old placard picked up in New Orleans that advertised
Princess Zina—whose method of divination was "flowerscopes,"
who might have read your fortune in bougainvillea blossoms
and birds of paradise from a stall in Jackson Square, for a fee.

In the study a few steps up from the salon, a recamier stretched
out in the center of the room, dressed lavishly in cushions and
coverlets, under a ceiling from whose center cascaded a tent-like

canopy of silk panels. At the back of the room, a glass curio cabinet contained a collection of skulls—wooden, beaded, clay, ivory, metal. "I am fighting a war against minimalism," Bill liked to say, "and winning."

More marvels filled the small kitchen: the massive, brass-hinged oak apothecary cabinets Ellen discovered on the side of a road in the Catskills, their shimmery old glass fronts still intact and hardware still in place; the delicate porcelain oyster plates side by side with sturdy French copper pans on the walls; the vintage industrial Wolf stove with six burners and a salamander at the top, which I long suspected was leaking gas and might kill us all the next time someone lit a cigarette, or a joint, but, fuck it, what a way to go.

I scavenged and bargained and bought and bartered and haunted the local thrift shops for things that would make my little apartment feel like a miniature version of the People's Palace, but also entirely my own. I stripped linoleum off floors and sanded and sealed the wide, softwood boards. I replaced ordinary doorknobs with antique ones, plastic light-switch plates with painted ceramic ones, lackluster lighting fixtures with a beaded Moroccan chandelier here and a Danish paper number there. I painted the bathroom walls delft blue and the ceiling the yellow of Van Gogh's sunflowers; the Dutchness I detected before moving in always maintained. I embarked on collections: small floral still lifes, and souvenirs related to Tintern Abbey, a place invoked in the title of my favorite poem. And I came to believe that how one felt about my apartment was a reliable measure of how one felt about me. *Love me, love my home.* Sometimes I brought home the sort of person who resented its repleteness and mistook it for clutter, who disliked its colorfulness and confused it with chaos. That such people were judging me, in the form of my apartment, was self-satisfyingly obvious to them; that I was judging them back, well, I doubt they had any notion.

I started to love that apartment so much that it grew painful to think of leaving it so soon. I had no choice but to stay and hope that I would come to love the neighborhood, too. I did.

I moved in as a twenty-five-year-old single woman who spent most of her time in bars. I lived there when I got to know Frank, a good and thoughtful man who loved cooking and loved Wordsworth, and not long after our first date, he moved in.

We lived there together when the planes hit the towers. And when, not long after, my father died. We got engaged there and married. There were dinner parties. Holiday parties. Cassoulets and rib roasts and shrimp boils. So much wine. Too many cigarettes.

Much laughter. Much love. And not the dissolution of love, but its shifts and tempers, its deviations and degrees.

Jobs in publishing, in social services, in academia, in bars and shops. No jobs at all. Years with plenty of money, years with next to none. At the kitchen table, I wrote a book. In my bed, I wrote another. We raised no children there, but the greatest of all cats.

I lived there when we separated, and when he got sick and we unseparated. In February, at thirty-nine, I became a widow there. And that's when it was time to move out, but I couldn't afford it. I was still there when I became motherless, too.

A few years later Bill and Ellen also died, and I helped to clean and empty and shut down the People's Palace—a dusty, dirty, difficult task that took many hands and many weeks. When I was sure I'd cleaned and priced what had to be the last tchotchke, the last pearl-handled demitasse spoon, the last Bakelite brooch, something else materialized from some closet, some drawer, some long-forgotten public-radio tote bag.

So much stuff. No end of stuff. And from it I inherited my favorite furniture and objects: Bill's scuffed and scarred glass-fronted barrister bookcases, some Persian rugs, the oyster plates, Princess Zina. My apartment became as much like theirs as it ever would—but also less my own. It looked exactly as I'd always wanted, but its energies and frequencies had altered. Every corner, every surface, exposed reminders of who was gone, where I'd never noticed anything before. The cat—she, too, was gone by then, but the phantom of her jumped on the bed many mornings, as if to wake me for its phantom breakfast.

Almost thirty years after I first visited Ireland, and after many more visits, a way in which I might move there presented itself. I had by then come to believe that to contend with loss, to grieve in a way I had not been able to manage at home in New York, I would have to be there. And not in Dublin or Belfast—in Glenarm.

I had been teaching nonfiction in an MFA program in creative writing since 2016. I had never gotten a degree in creative writing, and the only workshops I'd ever taken were in poetry, as an undergraduate. But I had run writing workshops for years before I started teaching at the university: in a senior citizens' day center, in an adult-education program, in a church, online, and at my kitchen table in Brooklyn. I have always loved teaching, and over time, I noticed that student writers were getting something valuable from the workshop experience: accountability, feedback, and a sense of writerly community.

The MFA program I taught in was a "low-residency" program: we all met in person, on campus, for ten days full of workshops, lectures, readings, and socializing before the start of each semester, and then did most of our work online. At one of our residencies, after an invigorating day of teaching and talking and listening, the idea started forming. *I wouldn't mind going back to school*, I thought. In fact, *I'd probably love it.*

It lingered with me throughout the week. I thought back to my afternoon in Belfast with Ciaran Carson, which had ended with a visit to the Seamus Heaney Centre at Queen's University in Belfast. Maybe I could go back to school there—and commute from Glenarm. I sent off an application.

I was forty-seven years old. I had published a book. I taught graduate students. Some of my friends thought the idea of my going back to school was ridiculous—more than one made cracks about Rodney Dangerfield—but I didn't. I don't think I'd impressed on them how I longed to return to Northern Ireland, especially to Glenarm, and that being a student would make that possible. But the more I thought about it, the more the prospect excited me. I waited to hear back, and got good news: I'd been accepted—and given a scholarship.

But even if I disagreed with the friends who brushed off the idea, my plan had flaws. I was not only broke, I was in debt. The scholarship would cover some of the cost but was a long way from covering all of it. I am also disorganized. Even simple forms turn my brain to sludge: one look at the visa application filled me with dread. I wasn't being realistic. But I'd already started day-dreaming about being on the learning side of a classroom again. Fresh notebooks and new pens! Crunchy autumn leaves on the small, pretty campus. And the possibility of a year in Glenarm. *A whole year.*

The day before I would have to complete and submit the visa application, I went to a museum with a friend. I was a tingling mass of raw nerves. I expected her to give me a pep talk and tell me to go for it. She didn't. Instead, over lunch, she suggested that I wait a year. Take some time to prepare and plan, to keep my head down and work, save some money. I sat there nodding in agreement with everything she said, gritting my teeth, hating that she was right and I knew it.

"I'm sure you can defer for a year, on the acceptance and the scholarship," she said as we walked to our different subways. She was right about that, too. I would keep my head down. I would work on a new book. And then, in 2019, I would go back to Northern Ireland and back to school. And I knew if I didn't make it happen then, I probably never would—and I would feel stuck, in the home where I'd lost my father, my mother, my husband, my aunt and uncle, my cat. It had been a beautiful home, but it was haunted. And I sensed that the grief I had postponed would never find solace until I left my ghosts behind, until I was in Ireland again.

My timing. In the big picture, I would be moving to Northern Ireland on the brink of the planned implementation of Brexit, which threatened the fluidity of the border between the North and the Republic of Ireland, which many believed also threatened the hard-won, sometimes fragile peace that had followed 1998's Good Friday Agreement, which had formally ended the Troubles and begun the peace process. In the smaller, more immediate picture: I had booked a flight that was scheduled to arrive in Dublin on September 7, 2019, but there was an airline strike, and the only other flight I could afford, and which would arrive in time for me to start school on schedule, was on the night of September 10, which meant I would arrive in Ireland on 9/11.

Like every New Yorker I know, I have intimate and painful associations with that day. The uncertainty, then the knowing, then the terrible feeling of loss, both pervasive and personal. The sights, the smells, the sounds, even the textures and tastes from that terrible time. It didn't seem like the most promising day to start a new life—if that's what I was hoping to do. I called on Seamus, who had been my driver when I was reporting on the Roger Casement story, to come and collect me, my two enormous duffel bags, and my suitcases at Dublin Airport that morning. My flight landed just before 5 a.m. By the time I made it through passport control, claimed my luggage, and exited the airport, it was nearly 7.

While Seamus loaded up the car, I stood firmly on the pavement. *I am here. In Ireland again.* And this time I'd be staying for a while. I knew this was true, but I couldn't believe it. Bleary as I was, I couldn't nap at all during the two-and-a-half-hour drive north to Glenarm. I had done this thing, this thing that had been impossible a year earlier, and I had to be awake for every second of the ride. When we were about twenty minutes north of Dublin, the sun rose, and suggested that it would be a bright day, a good day. Soon after we crossed the border into Northern Ireland, Seamus stopped at a gas station and got himself a cup of tea and a coffee for me. I could see and think more clearly. This was real: this gas station, this car, this coffee, this road that would take me to Glenarm.

My exhilaration didn't last long. We pulled up in front of the house—the same house I'd rented in 2017—and emptied my belongings from the back of the car. I thought Maureen, the house manager, said the door would be unlocked—but it wasn't. And I didn't want to call her so early. We loaded up the car again; Seamus didn't want to leave me with my luggage, locked out. The hotel in Carnlough, one village north, was open for breakfast, and by the time we finished and returned to Glenarm, I figured someone would have unlocked the door.

It was still locked. We drove to the village's visitor center, hopeful that someone there could help me. It wasn't open yet. But a man stood outside, taping a flyer to the front door. "It's not usually open this early," he said, almost apologetically.

He asked what I was doing in Glenarm, and I told him I was doing a master's program in creative writing at Queen's—but I didn't want to live in Belfast, I wanted to live *here*. Colin told me he was a storyteller, and that he'd come to the visitor center to drop off flyers about the upcoming Glens Storytelling Festival—and that now that I lived here (or would live here, as soon as I could get into my house), I should come. While we chatted, I felt a sharp, electric pinch on my left hand, a wasp. I winced. Colin asked if I was alright, and I said I'd be fine.

"Where are you staying?"

"One of the village houses, in Toberwine Street." The house

was known as a village house because it had been bought by the village committee in the '80s, in poor condition, with the help of subsidies and grants to restore it.

"Did you ring Maureen?"

"I tried. No answer."

He introduced himself to Seamus, and said, "Follow me." We trailed his car up an unfamiliar road into the hilly farmlands on the outskirts of the village. Maureen walked toward us as she saw us approaching. An emergency veterinarian had just arrived, to tend to one of her bulls who'd had a medical emergency that morning.

"I'm so sorry, Maureen," I said. "But I thought the door would be open."

"It is," she said, with certainty. "The back door."

The back door. Of course. Wow, I felt stupid, and guilty for bothering Maureen at home in the midst of a livestock emergency. Of course she'd meant the back door; she expected we'd drive to the parking space behind the house, which is exactly what we should have done. I apologized again, and Seamus and I followed Colin back into the village, where he patiently guided us to the back of the house.

I thanked him. "No bother," he said. "You should take care of that wasp sting."

Seamus helped me load my stuff into the house, and we said goodbye. I shut the door behind him, rooted through my backpack to find the tube of Neosporin I'd had the foresight to stuff into a Ziploc bag along with my toothpaste. I washed my wasp-stung hand, squeezed some salve out of its tube, and looked around the kitchen. I remembered making fish tacos there in 2017, and gratin dauphinois on a rainy summer's day. I walked through to the dining room. I hadn't lived in a place with a dining room since I was a teenager. Then into the living room, with its two deep window seats and a fireplace with a cast-iron surround. This would be *home*, not just for a month, but for a whole year.

I stepped back outside, into the backyard and garden. I'd never had a backyard or a garden since I was a teenager, either. I noticed that one of the whiskey-barrel planters was full of fresh herbs—sage and mint and parsley, and knelt down to inhale, and as I exhaled, the morning's trials dispersed into the fresh, clear air of the glens. *It would be okay. It would all be okay.*

A knock on the front door. It was Penny, the person I'd known longest in Glenarm, who had managed the Barbican when I stayed there in 2016. She had come to welcome me back, and to invite me to a surprise birthday lunch for Maureen, at the Water's Edge café opposite the beach. Not only had I interrupted Maureen—for no good reason—during the emergency vet's visit to her farm, I'd done it on her birthday. I might have been the last person she'd want to see at lunch, but I accepted the invitation. And Maureen didn't seem dismayed by my presence there. There was soup, and quiche, and cake, and friendly banter among the guests, some of whom I recognized from my earlier visits to the village, others whose faces were new to me.

Afterward, I took my first walk on Glenarm's beach since my previous visit. The stones were as perfectly smooth as I remembered them—the most beautiful stones I'd ever seen on a beach, I thought in 2017, and I still thought so. I had the beach to myself. The day was clear enough that I could see Scotland.

Then I went to the marina, where I saw a boat called *Moonlight* returning to harbor, two fat seals, one gray, one white, sunning themselves on the rocks, a rusty old barge called *Pussycat*—and I asked it, *What's new?* And then I walked back through the village, up the Vennel and Spring Hill, past the broken-down former parochial hall, boarded up and mostly hidden by ivy, to the path called the Layde Walk, whose altitude makes for sweeping views of the sea, the castle, and the forest. There are benches along the trail, and I stopped to rest. I felt the cold bronze dedication plaque at my back, and turned to read it: *In loving memory of Wee Lily. She left paw prints on our hearts.*

Later, my friend Jacky came by to say hello; she knew that I loved to cook, and it was she who had planted the herbs in my backyard, so they'd be ready for me on arrival. It was also she who'd let me know that the green Georgian house on Toberwine Street was available to rent, and who'd told Maureen I was returning to Northern Ireland and would love to stay here again.

Still later, Mark came up from Belfast to help me unpack. We ordered Chinese food from a takeaway in Carnlough, and worked late into the night. The next morning, we took the bus into Belfast together, and after we said goodbye, I registered for my classes, went to orientation, and was a student again, a few months before my forty-ninth birthday. I felt almost as excited as I had thirty years earlier, on my first day of college—I had left home, I was starting something, I had been given a chance to learn more, and maybe to live better. On my bus ride back to Glenarm, a rainbow arced over Ballygally beach, and I thought again, *It will all be okay.* The planning and postponing and waiting and packing, the saying goodbye to my home of more than twenty years and the city where I was born and raised, to the friends and family I love, had not been done wastefully, without purpose and intention.

I'd had less than a month to clear out my apartment before I moved to Glenarm. And when I told people—friends, acquaintances, coworkers, family—that, yes, I was finally leaving, the first thing most asked was: *What are you doing with your apartment?* Which is the New Yorkiest possible reaction. Any other details, or questions, or well wishes could come later.

I considered subletting. I considered letting a friend move in. But I knew that I was ready to let it go. And when I told my friends, acquaintances, coworkers, family that that's what I was going to do, most said, in one way or another, *You're crazy.* When and if I returned from Ireland, I was warned, I'd never find such a good deal again. Maybe that's true—but I knew that if I ever wanted to move back to New York, I would find a way.

At the same time, I was surprised, and moved, by how much more sentimental about my apartment, and my stuff, my friends were than I was. In the weeks before I left, many came over to help me pack the small portion of things I had decided to keep (I'd crammed a lot into those 450 square feet): some kitchen gear, a few hundred books, some paintings and small pieces of furniture. They helped me clean. They helped me run moving-out sales. They helped me lug junk to the curb. And although it was strange, even shocking, to see how quickly what had taken me two decades to fill with things that gave me pleasure, to make a home, could be emptied, it didn't make me sad. I was happy to be leaving, and I was ready. I was more than ready—I was late; it should have happened sooner.

But even though it didn't make me sad, it did make me remember an incident that had stung me, once, long ago, maybe two years after I'd moved in.

An adventurous friend had come to visit. He had lived in the Amazon rainforest in his youth. He had lived in a village on the Nile as an adult. He had wandered. He had never settled. For someone who was great fun, he had an ascetic streak. Material possessions meant nothing to him. Faith mattered to him, and friendship. Not stuff.

He came over for coffee one afternoon. He hadn't seen the apartment since right after I'd moved in—when he had turned up to install a mezuzah on my doorpost, which I had not asked him to do, but I did not stop him—and by then I was proud of the place. I showed him around.

"It's *so nice*," he said, and I was overjoyed. But his expression quickly hardened, and he added: "I find it depressing."

Shame filled me like a cold, heavy liquid, and I was too ashamed to ask him what he meant. But I believed it had something to do with my love for my things, that this was a shallow love, and that my attachment to them was wrong. I said nothing but searched in my thoughts for support and consolation. There were memories of Bill and Ellen, who loved things, but who had done so much for others. There was William Morris, whose ideas and productions I relied on to confirm my hope that style *was* substance, not in conflict with it. I had filled my home with things that I knew to be beautiful and believed to be useful. And if perhaps I had persuaded myself that some of those things were useful only because they were beautiful, that was fine.

They are only things, I remember telling myself, after my friend had issued his judgment. *And although I love them, I could live without them.* Afterward, I sometimes wondered if I'd told myself the truth.

5

GLENARM—THE PLACE THAT SEDUCED ME AWAY
from New York City after a lifetime there—is a village about thirty
miles north of Belfast on the coast of County Antrim. It's an old
place, some say the oldest town in the province of Ulster, which
includes the six counties that make up Northern Ireland and three
in the Republic of Ireland. It is home to about six hundred people.

Glenarm is also the name of the slim ribbon of a river that
rushes through the village after heavy rains, and is sometimes as
still as bathwater, choked as it is, in places, by knotweed. The invasive plant probably arrived in Glenarm sometime in the twentieth
century. The Vikings, the Normans, the English, and the Scots all
got here long before that. On bright clear days, you can see Scotland from the coastline that is the village's eastern edge: there's the
Mull of Kintyre in the foreground, there are the peaks of the Paps
of Jura farther out.

And Glenarm is the name of the protected 441-acre forest one
enters after passing through a high stone arch where the village's
main street ends, after it has turned from Toberwine Street into
Altmore Street, where it widens into a nearly perfect Georgian

period-piece film set—save for the cars and vans and trucks parked beside the narrow sidewalks and the faded red "British" telephone booth—after the street has passed Castle Street, at the end of which, over a small bridge, across the river, looms the gatehouse to the castle that is also called Glenarm.

Glenarm village, river, forest, castle: no thing is just one thing up here, out here.

The name Glenarm means, too, that it is a glen—a valley, a long green trug shaped by the surrounding hills. It is the southernmost of nine glens that together make up the Glens of Antrim, the first glen, or the last glen, depending on which way you're going. The region is designated by the Northern Ireland Environment Agency as an AONB—an area of outstanding natural beauty.

They are not mistaken, these Northern Irish Environmental agents. It really is naturally beautiful here. Outstandingly so.

There's a preschool housed in the Orange Hall—the gathering place for the local lodge of the Orange Order, the Protestant loyalist fraternal organization best known for its annual march on the twelfth of July—an event undeniably martial in nature, which commemorates the victory of the Protestant king William of Orange over the Catholic King James at the Battle of the Boyne in 1690. There's a primary school—Seaview—for children aged four through eleven.

Seaview Primary School is also where a small, devoted group of women who range in age from about eighteen to nearly eighty gathers on Tuesday evenings for Sue McBride's yoga class, hours after the children have gone home. It is also where, when I stayed in the village for a month in 2017, I made some of the friends here to whom I am closest.

That summer, I sometimes saw a man, only the one, in the yoga class. He'd arrive seconds before Sue, who grew up in Liverpool, started gently instructing us in her soft Scouse, and would leave right after he'd snapped out of savasana, risen from the dead, as soon as the class has ended. He never said a word, and I suspected that he was secretly doing yoga. I supposed it was a secret because being a man in a yoga class is not a thing that's done here, in this glen. But maybe I was wrong. Glenarm's not too small to surprise expectations, to subvert presumptions; no village is. It is best, I remind myself, to presume nothing.

After Sue's yoga class many of us would go to Stevey's pub, the Bridge End Tavern, for drinks and chat, because a very civilized thing about Ireland is that after yoga, you go to the pub. "Here come the pole dancers," Stevey sometimes couldn't help saying when we stepped inside with our mats.

In 2019, I moved back into the house I'd stayed in that summer. It's like many other houses in the village, a Georgian row house. Its façade is painted a pale minty green, the front door is a darker, piney green. It's more house than I've lived in since I was a child.

After decades of apartment living in fewer than five hundred square feet, of putting up guests on my living room sofa, of schlepping to a Laundromat one morning every weekend, this house, which is a fine and sturdy old house, but which I don't think anyone here would call extraordinary, feels almost like a mansion to me. Three bedrooms: I have slept in all of them, because why not. *Two toilets!* I use both, because I can.

I live near a castle. I have a fireplace. A washing machine. A dishwasher. I have a garden, where I grow lettuce and kale, arugula and tatsoi. All this, at about a third of what my rent ran in Park Slope, which was, by Brooklyn standards, a steal.

I can hear my dead mother saying: *You get what you pay for.*

And I can hear her saying: *Location, location, location.*

Even at her worst, even with all the medication, even after the psychotic break that was, I think, the beginning of her end, she always had something to say. Why wouldn't she now, after she's gone?

There were once many hotels in Glenarm—the Antrim Arms, Drumnagreagh, Farmer's, the Seaview—and now there are none. Every hotel had a pub, and there were many more besides: I've heard about the Barbican. McNeill's, O'Boyle's, the Heather Dew, the Greyhound.

All the butcher's shops are gone, too: McAuley's and McAllister's, and Mulvenna's. It's hard to imagine now that there were ever enough people here to buy so much meat.

In the memories of some of the older villagers, those who were born and raised here, Glenarm had two drapers' shops, a hardware store, Irvine's grocers, Pullen's grocers, two sweets shops, a garage, even a cinema. You can still see the dim, spectral signage left behind by a business where you could have bought a boat, or could have had your boat repaired. Glenarm, I have read, and have been told, was the busiest, and most prosperous, village on the coast.

You didn't need to go anywhere for anything, Mona Hyndman, who worked in the only grocery shop in the village now, told me. Everything you needed was right here. As a girl, Mona played tennis on a court on the castle side of Glenarm Forest. I've looked for vestiges of the tennis court, any signs that it was there, and have found none.

The building that last housed a post office in Glenarm still stands, with the words "Post Office" still inscribed in faded paint above its door, but no one has mailed or collected a letter or parcel there since 2011.

A bank stood at the crossroads where Toberwine Street and Altmore Street and the Vennel intersect, which used to be the center of Glenarm, and that's gone, too. There is no cash machine in the village.

And when almost no businesses remained, it was then, I have heard, that, for some of those who'd held out and held on, the time had come to get out, move elsewhere, move on. But some people, like Mona, would never live anywhere else, and would never want to. She's active on the Village Committee, full of pride in, and love for, Glenarm.

What's left?

Two pubs. There's one some call the Catholic one—Stevey's, the Bridge End Tavern, and the other that some call the Protestant one—the Coast Road Inn—which sit side by side. They are not strictly segregated, not at all. (Presume nothing, I remind myself.)

In the Vennel, a pretty side street that leads up to Spring Hill, whose name comes from a Scottish word for alley, there's a shoebox-sized pharmacy that opens for a few hours most mornings and most evenings.

Five doors from my house, there's the shop where Mona used to work, where I buy milk and onions and newspapers and sometimes too many packets of crisps, especially when I'm on deadline or can make some other excuse, which I always can. And the shop used to give you cash back if you spent at least five pounds with your bank card, which made the absence of an ATM in the village alright. They don't give cash back anymore. Not that there's much I need cash for here—other than for pints at Stevey's pub.

On the grounds of Glenarm Castle, there's a shop stocked with fancy soaps and cashmere throws and artsy jewelry, and a tea-room open for lunch. Since I've moved here, more commerce has sprung up on the grounds: there's a visitor center where you can buy steaks and roasts of the local beef (the excellent Glenarm Shorthorn), and smoked, vacuum-packed slices of the local organic salmon, chocolates, and, in the spring and summer, potted plants and flowers. A "pizza pavilion" that closes early and is only open on the weekends. Same goes for the ice cream parlor. A pottery studio. A shop that sells upcycled furniture, cards, Christmas ornaments.

The castle is its own small world inside another small world. It is essential to the life of this village and it is also set apart from it. The tourists who come to visit its walled gardens, with a topiary maze and espaliered fruit trees, who come for the tulips and the annual Dalriada music festival, or to have a cup of tea and a toilet break on their way to the Giant's Causeway, can get there without even knowing the village exists. When you approach Glenarm from Larne or Belfast or anywhere farther down the coast, you come to a roundabout. One spoke will take you to the castle. Another continues up the shore. The least traveled is the one that leads into the village.

I don't drive. No train stops here. A bus loops along the curvy coastal road from one village to the next, and the next, and then back the other way, a few times a day, but never on Sunday. If I take the bus to Larne, the biggest town between here and Belfast, I can connect to another bus that will take me into the city; the journey takes an hour and a half. If I have something to mail, I take the bus one stop in the other direction, to Carnlough, which, compared to Glenarm, feels downright cosmopolitan, with a sprawly old hotel, two Chinese takeaways, a doctors' office, a library, and a smart, airy coffeehouse that would look right at home in Park Slope.

Location, location, location. But for all the village lacks in commerce, in amenities, in mod-cons, I still think my mother, who spent her childhood summers on Fire Island and never stopped loving and longing for the sea, would get Glenarm, and love it, too. And I would tell her not to worry: every self-respecting village in the North, no matter how small, has a hair salon. Even Glenarm. It is my casual observation that the people of Northern Ireland are among the vainest in the world. (I would not tell her that I still cut my hair maybe twice a year, that I still can't be bothered.)

I would tell her I am doing fine. And I would tell her I am happier here, happier now.

Don't worry. Rest.

"Toberwine Street?" I can hear my mother saying. "Leave it to you to find the only street in Ireland with a Jewish name."

This has not gone unnoticed by me, nor unremarked on by friends back home.

Toberwine. As in: "Dr. Toberwine is an excellent cardiologist. He went to Harvard." Or: "I cried when Toberwine's closed down. They had the best pastrami in Flatbush."

"*Toberwine?*" a skeptical friend asked.

"Yes, Toberwine. Weird. I know."

"It sounds . . ."

"Jewish. Yes. I know."

"It's Gaelic? Irish? *Really?*"

"So I have read."

"What does it mean?"

"I'm not sure," I say. "An Irish place-name website says it might mean 'green well.'"

"Green well? That's kind of nice."

"The website also says it might have something to do with warts. That the water from the well was said to cure warts. So . . ."

"You live on Wart Street."

"It is possible that I live on Wart Street."

If this etymology seemed undignified to me at first, it no longer does. I have come to love it, and to hope that it's true.

I have read elsewhere that Toberwine translates to "the sweet well of the saddles"—whatever that means—but I like the wart story much better.

Toberwine. Oy!

It is possible that I am the only Jew around—there aren't many in all of Northern Ireland, even in Belfast—a strange state of affairs to someone born and raised in New York City, though perhaps less so to me than to those few bold and curious locals who have cared enough to try to tease out this information.

To have asked bluntly *What are you?* would have been a provocation here not so long ago. A man from Belfast told me it was the question he feared most when he was growing up. Now, there are subtler ways to get to it. There's a circling around, an indirect route.

"Was that you I saw at mass yesterday?" one of the old men at the Bridge End Tavern asked me one afternoon when I first arrived.

I shook my head no.

Two days later, the same man asked: was it me he saw leaving the Presbyterian church?

I shook my head again. "I'm glad you're sitting down for this," I said. "Let me get you your next pint."

He received the news with surprise. That I could be something other than Catholic or Protestant hadn't entered his mind. He took slow sips of his stout and went quiet. I did not detect any malice—only bewilderment. But in a gloomy cast of mind, this kind of thing, this kind of curiosity and this kind of questioning, even this kind of silence, makes me anxious, and I remember that I am, in more than one way, an outsider here, a woman on my own (at first) in a small, somewhat remote village. And I consider the very particular weight of religious identity in this country, and how crushing that weight has been, and might be again.

And sometimes, still gloomier, I think about mobs with pitchforks.

In a more cheerful mood, I fix my gaze across the North Channel toward Scotland and imagine myself as the heroine in a forgotten Sir Walter Scott novel called *The Jewess of the Glens*. She is courageous and clever, with thick black curls that flow from the crown of her heart-shaped head to the narrow of her long back. And she sings like a nightingale.

And I remind myself how good the people here, so many of the people here, have been to me, and are. They are kind. They have helped me, and they have made me feel at home in this village.

Don't worry, I want to say to my mother. *Rest.*

I'm good. It's good here.

It was to Stevey's pub that Penny McBride directed me when I first came to Glenarm on the tenth of July in 2016. An artist and weaver of willow baskets, Penny was also a manager at the Barbican, where I was staying. It had no television, and no Wi-Fi, and this is a great part of its appeal—when there isn't a game you want to watch.

I asked Penny if there was anywhere in the village where I could see the European Cup final that evening. They'd be showing the match at the Baptist hall, she told me. "And at Stevey's pub."

A long pause followed, my first taste of Penny's immaculate comic timing. And then, her delivery, impeccably dry: "I think you might have more fun at the pub."

It's a place where men, and sometimes, but not often, a woman or two, spend their afternoons drinking beer and sometimes talking *a lot*, and sometimes very little. Where the occasional tourist stops in for a pint and a bit of local color. Soccer matches and quiz shows play on the big TV; people here are serious about both pastimes. On weekends, especially if a big game is on, it can be packed. Its low ceilings are supported by rough wooden beams, nautical bric-a-brac on the window ledges reminds us that we are by the sea, and a coal fire often glows in the hearth. Twelve stools are stationed at the L-shaped bar; upholstered benches line the walls. Upstairs, the village book club holds its monthly meetings. Out back, there's a courtyard where people smoke—and take in the sunshine on warmer, clearer days.

It is unassuming and cozy; to my mind, an ideal village pub. And at £3.50 a pint, its Guinness is a bargain—Stevey doesn't want to hear about a cheaper pint anywhere in the county and will not be outdone for value. It's also some of the best I've drunk; I speculate that this is because the line that runs from the keg to

THE SLOW ROAD NORTH

the tap is uncommonly short, traveling through a hole drilled into the bar's back wall to a storage area in the yard, where it keeps it a steady, cool, outdoor Glenarm temperature.

Under a different name, it was also the pub where, in 1854, cholera broke out and proceeded to kill off a good portion of Glenarm's population. Many of those who died in that epidemic are buried in the graveyard of St. Patrick's church, around the corner, beside the harbor. Some of the old gravestones have darkened almost to black and settled down among the weeds and grass at a slovenly tilt, like broken, rotted teeth. Graveyard, plague yard: the scene is melancholic and not a little mad, and exactly my sort of thing—picturesque decay, Late Romantic ruin. I find it very beautiful.

So much of this village, I will see in time, is elegiac, scattered with memorials, formal and informal, to what once was here, and now is long gone.

Stevey's pub is not just a pub: it is also a sweets shop, and it is here to which the children bound after school for fistfuls of gummy, sweet, sour, fizzy treats. Some of the children seem just a little afraid of Stevey, who, I suppose it must be said, might not have the look of a nice man. He could be a boxer. A bouncer. A pirate.

Some adults seem a little bit scared of him, too. But he is also a funny and witty man, who looks just tough enough to keep a cheeky child in line, to keep order in a village pub when order must be kept. He has been kind to me. And he knows how much his pub matters to its patrons, especially the men who drink there every day. Like all great pubs, it is also a community center, a hub for news and stories. And I haven't met many people who work as hard as Stevey, who is at the Bridge End every day, from noon to midnight, and has been for more than forty years—since he wasn't much older than a child himself.

Up here a "taxi driver" is never only a taxi driver.

I have heard about a cook who sometimes drives locals to the Belfast airports. I've heard about another taxi driver in a nearby village who is also an undertaker, a pairing too charged with the potential for a terrible punch line for me to seek out his services—either of them.

And there was the friendly, chatty farmer who drove me to Cushendall one June evening when I wanted to hear Irish music at Johnny Joe's pub there. I squeezed in beside him in his small car and he started for the Coast Road.

"Where in the states are you from?"

"New York."

He might have guessed. He had lived in New York, or near New York, long ago and not for long, when he was young.

"What are you doing *here*?" he asked. "Glenarm is the town that time forgot."

I told him I was here because I want the forest and I want the sea and Glenarm does not force me to choose between them; it gives me both. I am here, I said, because, *come on*, it's so beautiful here. That was the truth, but not all of the truth.

I did not tell him: I am here to grieve. For my mother, and for my husband. Because I have done a very poor job of it, and I would like to try again.

I did not say to him: I am also here—here in this village that looks to some like it's been left for dead—to live. I am here for the long-gone well that heals the wounded.

6

NOT TEN DAYS INTO MY LIFE IN GLENARM IN 2019, and I had already become the lowest of the low, the very worst thing a person here can be: *a grass.*

That's the colorful way they say "snitch" on this side of the Atlantic. *Say Nothing*—the title of Patrick Radden Keefe's brilliant 2018 book about the Troubles, gives some sense of how deep-seated the cultural expectation here is that one will keep one's mouth shut when faced with transgressions both large and small. Keep your head down, mind your own business, and hope that the disturbance in question will pass without need of any intervention from a busybody such as yourself.

When I say I snitched, I don't mean that I went to the police. That would have been an overreaction. Instead, I went to Maureen, my house's manager, a woman of tremendous energy and humor, whom I count as one of Glenarm's grandes dames, active with various village events and committees, in charge of its visitor center, knowing and known to all, and, it seemed to me, attuned to and aware of everything that goes on here. My reason for snitching falls into the minor misdeeds category; I received no threats, and I had not been harmed. But I had been annoyed. Very annoyed.

This is what happened. It started on my second Friday night in the village while I lay in bed reading, in the front-facing up-stairs bedroom. Just after ten, I heard a *rap-rap-rap* on my front door, and maybe because it was nighttime, and I was alone, and I was reading "The Dead Fiddler," one of Isaac Bashevis Singer's dybbuk-haunted stories—that Poe and his raven sprang to mind. *Suddenly there came a tapping.* I tightened my blankets around me. *Nevermore!*

I dog-eared my book, crept to the window, and looked down. There, in front of my house, stood three neck-tied-and-jacketed schoolboys, whom I estimated to be, on average, around age ten.

At that hour, it was unlikely that it was a visit from a welcom-ing committee. They hadn't brought flowers or homemade pies. Was something wrong? Had one of them been injured, and had they come to my door seeking help? If that was the case, I won-dered why they would choose my door, when there must have been plenty of people in Toberwine Street who were not strangers to them. Well, people do strange things in distress. I ran down the stairs. I opened the front door, and, as soon as I did, they fled.

I texted a neighbor to ask was this normal, this late-night door-knocking-and-running-away business? She gave no reply. Yes, I thought, *say nothing*, that's how it's done here.

And then my thoughts backed into the dim, dank corners that have always taken up too much space in my head, and that per-haps take up too much space in this country, too. Who were these kids? *To whom did they belong?* Could they, or at least one of their gang, be the offspring of the local leader of some or other paramilitary? This is the kind of thing one considers in this place, or at least the kind of thing I considered. (When I asked a friend in the village if I was crazy to think this way, she said I wasn't—"We all do.") To the small but warm and welcoming circle of friends I'd made in the village since my first visit, I had hoped to add some more. That I might also make some enemies was not a possibility I had ever considered.

I emailed Maureen, but didn't hear back from her immediately—not because she is a say-nothing kind of person herself, but because she's not a constant checker of email. She replied the next night, after I'd written to her once more, because it had happened again—the knocking and the running—earlier that evening, when I was making dinner. This time, it was a solitary perpetrator, one of the same boys who'd appeared the night before, on his own. Maureen was sorry to hear that this had happened, and said she'd have a word with the parents of those she thought to be the likely suspects. Another neighbor, she mentioned, had confronted a group of boys earlier. She would be vigilant, and would make it stop before it turned into a game.

Thanks, I figured, to her interventions, the knocking died down for a few weeks. A knock here, another there, not often. I decided to do what I'd normally do: say hello, smile, chat, be friendly. That seemed to disarm them, briefly. And ignoring them, which was what most people in the village with whom I discussed the problem advised me to do, didn't have much effect, either. I could put up with the nuisance, but it bothered me, not only because it disrupted my work, but because I felt that I'd been chosen because I was female, and living on my own, and an outsider, that they had picked me because I was a stranger. And when friends back home asked how things were, how I liked Glenarm, if it was as I had hoped it would be, I told them things were good, I liked Glenarm very much, yes, it was as I had hoped. "Only one problem," I'd say. The village boys. "Some of them can be a bit *Lord of the Flies.*"

They're just bored, I was told, and this sort of prank was, to them, just a diversion, just something to do. I'd speculated along those lines, too. To bored kids, my newness here was enough to make me a figure of interest. But anger sometimes flared up in me. Bored? Why should they be bored? They've got a whole forest down the street! They've got a beach full of treasures—sea glass and shells, driftwood and stones and fallen feathers and things left behind! They had no excuse for boredom.

But of course they did. They are bored, I reminded myself, because they are children, and children are often bored, regardless of resources—inner and outer. I was once a bored child, too, even in the madness of midtown Manhattan, even in the absolute chaos of the late 1970s. I had roller skates. I had disco. I lived in an apartment building full of other kids, and could walk to Central Park in five minutes. What business did *I* have being bored?

Yet I had my own shameful history as a miserable, and no doubt misery-making, adolescent prankster, and felt compelled to reflect on it. When I was about eleven, the company my mother worked for installed a telephone line in our apartment and paid for it, which, to my dumb, not-fully-formed brain meant that it was free, which it certainly was not. Whenever my mother went out for the night, I'd invite my best friend, Elizabeth, over, and we'd make a real party of it, setting up camp in the cramped home office with Cokes and bags of potato chips, dialing random numbers around the world, putting on an array of fake accents, most of which managed to come out sounding like Pepé Le Pew, no matter what region's tongue we thought we'd cannily represented. We were ridiculous, we were awful, and we were relentless. And when we'd tired of the random nature and global range of our efforts, we launched a more local and pointed campaign, directed at a French teacher at our school whom we despised. She was mean and sour and scowl-faced, and if she caught you chewing gum in class she called you a cow (*comme une vache, mademoiselle!*), but she did not deserve our hang-up calls, our nocturnal blasts of bombastic music, our petty cruelty.

One night, deep into our evening's entertainment, after this had gone on for many weeks, the phone rang—a thing that never happened, and which signaled to me that we were busted, and it was over. I answered, and on the other end was a deep-voiced New York City policeman from such-and-such special crimes division, asking for Liz and me by our names. He gave us a stern talking-to and warned that if it happened again, we'd go to court, and after that, it was very likely we'd be off to juvie, our lives destroyed before they'd ever really begun, and that it was nobody's fault but our own. We made no more calls, and never spoke of it again.

Years later, my season of crank-call criminality came up in a conversation with my mother. That was no NYC cop, she admitted. It was her friend Brian, who had been studying method acting at the time. Oh, he was good. And my mother, as usual, had been smarter and more attentive than I gave her credit for.

The kids started up again in early November, with a new, more self-assured aggression—not just knocking on the door, but sometimes kicking it, too. I thought of Martin Roper's novel, *Gone,* in which a Dublin couple sets out to remodel a house and is tormented by the children on their street, who throw rocks at their windows, call them increasingly foul names, and play a part in the collapse of their marriage. It hadn't been nearly so bad in my case, but I wondered if it would escalate. And I wondered if it was a rite of passage for Irish boys—the ones in the Dublin of *Gone*, the ones in the village where I lived.

"How are things in Glenarm?" friends back home continued to ask. "Great," I continued to tell them, except for the "Boys from the County Hell," per the Pogues song. One night, Maureen and her son pursued them into the forest, in the driving rain, and discovered who they were. She also found out that they'd been on a bit of a tear, that I was not the only one they'd bothered that evening, that a window at one of the churches in the village had been broken. I felt guilty for taking some comfort in this, in knowing I had not been their sole mark. But that their other targets were also vulnerable—elderly, or, like me, alone and female—confirmed my suspicion that they went after those who seemed the easiest marks, and that depressed me. "Miss Marple on the trail with knitting needles!" Maureen wrote to me, and I was grateful for her concern, and for her efforts. But it would probably lead to another cooling down, another temporary fix. Where was Brian the method actor now, when I needed him in Glenarm?

Deeper into autumn, I was too busy to be annoyed, or to let the annoyance get in my way. Work, as both student and teacher, had started to pile up—and I was not going to let Thanksgiving come and go without a celebration, without turkey and stuffing and cranberry sauce. I invited my four fellow American students from my master's program up to Glenarm for the occasion, and

Mark and our friend Paul, and a few locals, including Maureen, to join us later for desserts and drinks. The door-knockers were either deterred by the presence of so many people or the house was just so noisy and alive that no one noticed if they'd knocked.

At Christmastime, I put up an enormous tree that I'd lugged by taxi all the way from the Ormeau Road in Belfast—I'd waited too long and had missed a chance to get a tree more locally—and had a full house again. Katherine came all the way from New York to spend the holiday in Glenarm, and another American friend, Duley, whom I knew from my brief stint as a meat-monger in Brooklyn, traveled from Dublin where she had been living and volunteering in homeless services for much of the year. Mark was able to line up a few days off from the bar, so he came, too. His youngest sister, Joanne, drove him and their mother, Sheelagh, and Duley from Belfast, and presented us with the gift of an entire Serrano ham, which made not only for endless hors d'oeuvres, but also for irresistible photo ops with each of us cradling the hefty joint in turn—a profane pork pietà.

Sheelagh and Joanne returned to Belfast that night, leaving behind a cheerful, if unlikely, Christmas quartet: glamorous, professional Katherine; pierced and tattooed Duley, grumpy in affect but good-natured in spirit; and Mark and me, still uncertain about what our relationship was and where it might go. We all cooked well, and we all ate well: roasted racks of lamb on Christmas Eve, a standing rib roast with Yorkshire pudding and creamed spinach on the day itself, countless slices of Serrano ham, rum-soaked cakes, mulled wine. And when, as if on cue on Christmas morning, I woke to discover that every single heater in the house was as cold as the water in Glenarm Bay, that the heating oil had run out and I would not be able to get more until after Boxing Day, the four of us huddled together in the living room around the warmth of the fireplace, in the glow of the tree, watching *Father Ted* and *Derry Girls* and playing cards, a calm and cozy scene, happy.

Duley soon returned to Dublin, and Mark to Belfast, but Katherine lingered a few days longer with me in Glenarm. On her last night, we went to Stevey's pub and had a few drinks. When we returned to the house, a group of kids, most of whom I could identify as door-knockers, had clustered outside, and seemed to want to put up a show of strength, to be in our way. It was dark by then, and with most of our neighbors' lights out for the night, the street was only dimly illuminated. I fumbled for my keys, and then fumbled some more to fit the right one into the keyhole. "I can get you into your house," the oldest and tallest of the boys, the one I considered the leader of the pack, said. What did he mean? Had he gotten into my house before?

For the first time, I felt more than annoyed—I felt menaced. I was only on my own in the house two nights after Katherine returned to New York, but I couldn't sleep. And then I'd spend a night in Belfast before an early flight to London for a two-week work trip. Maureen assured me not to worry about the house while I was away—she'd keep an eye. I knew she meant it.

While I was in England, there was a meeting in the village about the kids. There would be more regular police patrols, and more contact with both the boys and their parents. After the meeting, they quieted down for a time. During that period of rapprochement, they were still on my mind, but I was not overtaken by anxious thoughts, nervous thoughts, or worries about when they might strike again. I thought instead about neighborliness, its graces, its gifts, its edges and limitations.

In Brooklyn, in the apartment I'd lived in for most of my adult life, I was the only tenant in a building otherwise occupied by the people who owned it. They had been good to me. They charged a much lower rent than I knew, and they knew, they could have. They were more than tolerant during the most financially unstable period of my life, the months after Frank died, when I neither worked nor paid my bills. I went for months without handing over rent checks, and received a gentle nudge in the form of a handwritten note on my doorstep. I liked them the first time we met—they were social workers who'd bought the building in the 1970s, when social workers could still afford to buy houses in Brooklyn—and, as the years passed, I came to love them. But although they came to my wedding, and they came to Frank's funeral, and left bags of basil and tomatoes from their garden on my doorstep, and I knew they were there for me, and they knew I was there for them, we didn't hang out much, or even really know each other well. We were polite, friendly, and cooperative with each other, while we kept at what felt like a healthy, civilized distance. Now that I am no longer in their house, I wish we had been closer. I wish that I had done more for them—that I had been more neighborly.

Together, we'd had our own troubles with a neighbor: a volatile man who owned a narrow alley beside our building, in which he kept up to three large guard dogs confined at a time, in which he sometimes lived in a lean-to he'd built at the back. When he lowered the fence that separated the alley from our house, the dogs would bark and sometimes even lunge at us when we walked up and down our stoop. More than once, I heard him mutter that he was going to burn our building down. More than once, he called my landlords vicious names. Neither they nor I could think of anything we'd done to provoke him. From time to time, his threats, and his dogs, created genuine terror, and unhappiness, for us all. At one crisis point, when I felt unsafe in my own home, I considered moving in with my half sister in New Jersey, just to get away from him.

And while the lads here in Glenarm had not caused me the kind of dread my old neighbor in Brooklyn did, they made me reconsider my expectations of the village, and of what life here would be like. I had convinced myself that I was coming to this place with clear eyes and without illusions, knowing that it could not be counted on to be unblemished, without conflict, unfailingly hospitable. I knew from my earlier visits that Glenarm was depressed, that there's little in the way of work opportunity, that sectarianism sometimes still rises up. I understood that this is a real place, and that like all other real places, it could not possibly be perfect. But for all the clarity I thought I had cultivated, I had nonetheless managed to romanticize the place, to see it only as a solution to some old and lingering problems, not as the source of any new ones.

In time, when other new people moved into Glenarm, the boys shifted their attentions to them. And later still, the inevitable happened: they got older, and seemed to have outgrown their door-knocking phase, just as I—I swear—haven't made a prank call since I was twelve. The following summer, I noticed that some of the lads had taken up fishing: I'd spot them in the river, close to where it joins the sea, knee-deep in the water, casting their lines. I thought, that is exactly the kind of thing kids here should be up to—spending time outdoors, enjoying nature—and then caught myself for sounding patronizing, if only in my own head. When I was a child, New York City was just the place where I happened to live—nothing special, nothing I had chosen. It was much later, when I was in my late teens, that I came to appreciate my hometown's specialness, to make use of its resources, to take part in its joys. They drove me nuts, those kids, early in my life in Glenarm. But maybe they'd figured out what made their hometown special sooner than I'd figured out what made mine.

7

I'D LIVED IN GLENARM LITTLE MORE THAN A MONTH when I noticed the flyer taped to the village shop's window: there would be a meeting that week at Seaview Primary School about its plan to become officially integrated. The Council for Catholic Maintained Schools, which oversaw the school, had considered shutting it down because of low enrollment—and the effects on the village that such a decision would have were terrible to consider. Seaview is at the heart of the village, and the village's fragile future is interwoven with its fate. Glenarm was already considered dead by some of its own residents, and by many passers-through— but the closing of the school could really bury it. What would keep young families here? What would Glenarm's demographics look like within a few years?

Here, the meaning of "integrated school" is different from what it means in the United States. It is an institution that, in the words of the Northern Ireland Education Authority, brings "children and staff from Catholic and Protestant traditions, as well as those of other faiths, or none, together in one school."

In contrast to my feelings about the adolescents in the village—at least the ones who made up the *Lord of the Flies* gang—I found the primary school children polite, friendly, and, most of the time, downright adorable, but that's not why I wanted to go to the meeting. The meeting interested me beyond its immediate, local context: I understood that it not only meant something big to Glenarm, but also to the whole of this small country. I had come to agree with most people I've met here that academic integration is among the best ways forward for Northern Ireland, toward a less sectarian, more peaceful future, an important and effective way to foster friendship and understanding among children of different faiths (or none). In my own generation, the separation could be stark. Mark, who went to Catholic primary and secondary schools in Armagh, had never played with Protestant children, and did not have a single Protestant friend until he moved to Liverpool to go to university. One of his sisters told me that during her first week as a nursing student at Queen's University in Belfast, another young woman in her dormitory was astonished to see her leaving the shower room: "My da told me Catholics never washed," she said. Decades of segregated education had sent up high, thick walls between children—like the so-called peace walls of Belfast that separate Catholic neighborhoods from Protestant—that they might not surmount until adulthood, and in some cases, not at all.

I wanted to go to the meeting and learn. Although loss and grief had led me to Glenarm, isolating myself from the people in the village, hiding away in self-imposed solitude and cutting myself off from human society were not what I wanted from my life here. On the contrary: as much as it was possible in New York, I had sequestered myself in my unhappiness, slowly and carelessly frayed connections with old friends, closed ranks to a small and trusted circle. In Glenarm I wanted to open myself up again, to meet people, and to make myself useful, somehow, to the life of the village.

The isolation in which grief had confined me in New York was new, unbidden, alien—because community had, until then, always mattered so much to me. I have yearned for it, and I have tried to cultivate it, and I have sometimes harbored romantic notions about what it might mean and what it could be. When I dropped out of high school to follow the Grateful Dead around America, it was the community—even communal—spirit that I cherished most from that time in my life, more than the music. In the bars where I'd made myself a regular in my twenties and thirties, again, the most powerful draw for me was the camaraderie I found in them. I've often daydreamed about communal living, too—despite the sobering, sometimes harrowing, stories I'd heard from friends who grew up on communes. And as I get older, and continue, almost certainly irreversibly, to be childless, I suspect that later in life I will seek out cohousing of some kind.

At the start of this millennium, I worked for two years for a grassroots anti-hunger nonprofit agency in New York. I loved telling people my job title—community organizer—and explaining what it meant to those who did not already know. I read and reread and highlighted and underlined the social justice activist and theorist Saul Alinsky's book *Rules for Radicals: A Pragmatic Primer*, and solicited stories and advice and wisdom from anti-poverty movement old-timers, most of whom encouraged my enthusiasm but also braced me for disappointment, urging me to lower my radical expectations, and temper my idealism—sometimes echoing and sometimes refuting Alinsky's lessons in their first-hand, experiential accounts. "If you want to get anything done, it comes down to building consensus," I remember one weary but still committed elder activist telling me, "and that means always playing the middle." Only a few weeks into the job, I understood what he meant: there were gains, but they always came with compromises. My expectations were lowered, my idealism tempered, and I was often frustrated—but my essential belief in community-building remained, and even grew stronger.

But community is really something else in Northern Ireland.

I have never before heard the word spoken as often as it is here, in political speeches, on the morning radio chat shows and the local evening news, in casual and formal and overheard conversations. More important, I have never heard it uttered the *way* it is here—hissed like a curse, or mumbled like a reluctant apology, sometimes slowly, sometimes fast, and always sounding like it isn't really the right word, the meant word, the truthful and unambiguous word.

Before I moved here, Mark sent me a YouTube link to a sketch by the English comedian Harry Enfield, both for my amusement and as a handy political gloss. In it, Enfield plays a character called William Ulsterman—a figure after the fashion of that notorious twentieth-century Ulsterman, the firebrand pastor and Unionist politician Ian Paisley, a tall and imposing slab of a figure—charismatic, sometimes funny, often frightening, and, throughout much of his career and presence in the Northern Irish public sphere, divisive and arguably quite dangerous.

Drawn with the broad strokes of sketch comedy, Enfield's William Ulsterman lacks the charisma of his model, but the Paisley-esque rhetoric is obvious. At a Christmas party, William is offered canapés by his pleasant host. Unimpressed by her friendliness and her mini-quiches, he tells her with indignation: "For hundreds of years my community has enjoyed cheddar cheese and pineapple on a stick, and today ye have been seen to trample our demands contemptuously." Near the end, he tells her to burn in Hell, and then she walks away, flummoxed. But another character unmistakably meant to parody one of Paisley's nemeses, longtime Sinn Féin leader Gerry Adams, gets the last word, to show, I assume, that bloated and disingenuous oratory does not belong exclusively to one side—that is, to one *community*.

Belfast writer Glenn Patterson wrote about Northern Ireland's special way with "community" in "Don't Mention the C-word," a 2014 essay for the *Irish Times*. When asked to speak at a seminar on the subject of community the previous year, he "thought twice—actually three or four times—before saying yes." He goes on to describe the ubiquity, the slippage and slipperiness of the word, and how they came to be: "In order to take the sectarian heat out of our conflict (another C-word in need of examination) the labels Catholic and Protestant were first diluted by the addition of 'community' and then effaced almost completely as the Protestant and Catholic communities became just the Two Communities."

I have become leerier, and more careful, with the word "community" since I moved here, but I see some value in its use as a replacement for either "Catholic" or "Protestant": it is, not intentionally, a reminder that the divisions here are not about religion alone, even if that's how the rest of the world tends to see them. They are also about class and civil rights, colonization, money, resources, history, power.

In some ways, I have also generally become more guarded in my own speech, more cautious with my choices of conversation subjects, and even words. Throughout this book, I have used "Ireland," "Northern Ireland," and "the North" to describe where I live. I have become comfortable using all three descriptors. But this, too, is fraught: in a pub in Belfast, the same one where Mark and I met, a man once told me I "should be shot" for saying "Northern Ireland." As a Republican, his preference would be "the North of Ireland."

But as complex, and charged, as language here can be, the way people use it in everyday life is one of my favorite things about this country, by any name. No matter how long I live here, I will never acquire a Northern accent—whenever I try to impersonate it, I sound like a character from South Park. But I have found many of the local words and idioms too wonderful not to absorb. "Melter"—a tedious and annoying person, so much so that he or she makes your head melt. "Dead on"—exactly right. "Catch yourself on"—don't be ridiculous (or self-aggrandizing). "Wise up"—get real. "Class"—so good, really really good.

About twenty people gathered in Seaview's small gymnasium for the meeting. There were some familiar faces, like Mona's. I saw Hilary, the child psychiatrist who lives across Toberwine Street from me and who sits on the school's board. Before I sat down in a molded plastic chair in the middle row, I took off my coat and pulled a notebook and pen from my tote bag. An older couple whom I'd not yet met sat behind me and introduced themselves. They were Frances and Jackie Wilson, I noted, in their eighties, smartly and colorfully dressed, radiating warmth and good humor. Whatever else might happen during the hour or so ahead of us, I was already glad I had come because, at the very least, I got to meet these lovely people.

An energetic and bright young teacher presided over the meeting. Apple-cheeked and quick-witted, Ashleigh Moran laid out the plan and the process: Seaview's bid for official integration would have to make its way through numerous official bodies before a decision would be made, and it was important to gather support from the village, both in the form of a petition and in personalized letters.

But even in the short time since the plan had been announced, interest in the school had soared—and enrollment for the next term was already up. That the plan would be approved was by no means a done deal, but I felt a swell of optimism. And if the plan succeeded, Seaview would make history by becoming the first Catholic school in Northern Ireland to integrate formally. As the village's only primary school, Seaview had already educated non-Catholic students, but other parents in the village opted to enroll their children outside of Glenarm instead, in Protestant schools.

When the meeting was over, I introduced myself to Ashleigh, and thanked her. I caught Frances and Jackie before they left, and told them how good it was to meet them.

"We hope we'll see you again," Jackie said.

I hoped to see them again, too, as soon as I could.

At home later that night, I felt that if the integration plan succeeded, there was plenty of hope for this "dying" village, this town that time had forgotten. I thought it would make a great documentary, or podcast. I found it fascinating, and I was sure that others would, too—and not only here in Northern Ireland. In the school's assembly room, I saw the cast of characters, other than the schoolchildren themselves, who would have key roles—young and old, native to Glenarm and newer to the village, Catholic and Protestant and neither. And although I now know her well enough to guess that this would make her laugh, in Ashleigh Moran I saw a natural and irresistible heroine, the central force around which the story's energy would gather. I knew I wouldn't make a documentary or podcast, but I still wanted to know more about Seaview, and integrated education, and Ashleigh herself.

We met for cake and coffee one afternoon in the courtyard of the Water's Edge café. Ashleigh's connection to Seaview ran deep: born and raised in Glenarm, she is a third-generation Seaview graduate, having followed her father and her paternal grandparents there. "I have a long-running relationship with the school, and now my own children attend," she told me. Her husband, Sean, a chef, was born not far away in the majority-Protestant town Carrickfergus, but his family moved to mostly Catholic Carnlough during the Troubles. (Ashleigh was the first person I talked to for this book who brought up the Troubles without any prompting.)

I told her I was trying to understand the changes in Glenarm, from the bustling village Mona had described to me, the Glenarm of her youth—with its hotels and factories and butchers' shops and cinema and tennis courts—to what it was now. I pictured its decline as though watching it on film, seeing in one quick and seamless scene, one shop disappear—*poof!*—and then another, and another. But along with the shops, Ashleigh said, there were also events in the village that brought people together, which had also come to an end. "There was civic week, sometimes a fortnight, with activities all through the day for children—paper airplane competitions, football games." And until not so long ago—recently enough that Ashleigh's young daughters had experienced it as toddlers—there was "the old hiring fair," a party in Toberwine Street with Irish dancing and music and old-fashioned costumes. When I asked her why these traditions ended, she speculated that it had to do with bureaucracy, with regulations and insurance, how much it costs the local council to block the street and assign police to the event. How sad that a thick band of red tape had put an end to the festive, and inclusive, village fun.

Ashleigh got her first job at age thirteen, and was the first person in her family to go to college. She took a gap year to travel in Asia and teach in Thailand before starting her education course at St. Mary's University College in Belfast. The summer after her first year at St. Mary's, she went to Uganda, and taught there, too. In her second year, she participated in the EU's Erasmus student exchange program, and studied in Belgium, and in her third year, she went on another student exchange trip, to Israel and Palestine. For her fourth and final year, she moved to the Canary Islands, where she taught at a bilingual private school and, for someone so young, was "paid a huge amount," which made it possible to travel around Europe, all the way up to the Norwegian part of the Arctic Circle.

When she graduated that June, she didn't go straight home to Glenarm—even though she had returned every weekend during college in Belfast. She took a summer job in Bournemouth, England, and in August flew home to Northern Ireland—where she had four job interviews lined up. She was offered the first job she interviewed for, in Downpatrick, more than an hour's drive from Glenarm, where she and Sean wanted to live and start a family. Their first daughter was on the way, and Ashleigh was having a difficult pregnancy: "Most people put on weight when they're pregnant. I lost two stone." She couldn't keep any food down, and was admitted to a hospital where she was fed by a drip. By then, the long commute to and from Downpatrick had proved to be too much; she'd resigned from the position, and picked up substitute teaching shifts in and nearer to Glenarm. And when, not long after, a full-time job opened up at Seaview, she applied for it and got it.

Her own experience as a Seaview pupil had been mostly positive. She remembers her geography teacher fondly—his love for his subject showed, and he was one of those teachers who had a special connection with the kids. Ashleigh loved geography, too, and nature—a passion she attributes to her father, a fisherman who loves the sea and the great outdoors. In her time as a teacher at Seaview, the school has become a qualified "Forest School," a child-centered learning approach in which lessons are learned not by rote, or only by reading, but by experiencing the outdoors firsthand, and per Wordsworth, letting nature be your teacher. I have often seen Ashleigh and her young charges—ranging in age from seven to nine—counting stones and inspecting driftwood on the beach, and closely observing the birds and trees and flowers and insects in Glenarm Forest and Straidkilly Nature Preserve, and whenever I see them, I think, *I wish my primary school had been more like that.*

Ashleigh takes care to explain that it was not necessarily bigotry that prevented many Protestant families (and nonreligious families) in the village from sending their children to Seaview. There were complex issues at play—and, as Ashleigh puts it, "really practical questions that made us look at ourselves and think about what would be the most inclusive way" of doing things. For example, Catholic children still prepare for sacraments, but they do it separately from the other children, so that Protestant and nonreligious and atheist kids aren't obligated to do something opposed to their, or their families', beliefs. In Ashleigh's childhood, Protestant families might have been uncomfortable with their children playing Gaelic sports, like hurling and camogie. Now, Seaview students learn about all of the world's major faith traditions. (I told her next time they discuss Judaism, I'll bring over some latkes.) And many of the children play both Gaelic sports and "English" ones, like soccer and rugby. Children, Ashleigh says, are "so much more accepting than adults." And to me, this truth is in itself a powerful argument for school integration. The numbers make a good case, too: in 2018, the year before the integration process began, Seaview's enrollment was 42. As I write this in 2023, Seaview has 109 students.

It was early in the pandemic when the pancakes first dropped through the mail slot in my front door: three of them, perfectly round and golden, neatly nestled in a small plastic bag, unaccompanied by a note.

"Mark," I hollered upstairs. "There are *pancakes* in the hallway."

I tried again, louder. "Did you see anyone at the door? Was there a knock?"

"No," he shouted back, and returned to whatever he was doing, as though it's perfectly normal for unexpected pancakes to pop through the postbox.

If such a thing had happened to me in Brooklyn, if a mysterious parcel of food landed in my mailbox with no note, I would have chucked it in the trash. But in Glenarm, I was sure the pancakes were perfectly safe. I slathered them in butter, anointed them with maple syrup, and quickly ate them all. Too bad for Mark.

Later that afternoon, I had a message from Frances, who'd befriended me on Facebook not long after the Seaview meeting. *Ah.* I told her I had no idea who'd made the pancakes, and thanked her. In the coming weeks, there would be more pancakes, and occasionally soup and bread and sweets, if she and Jackie had made a grocery run. I think they hadn't yet figured out that Mark had moved up to Glenarm from Belfast at the start of the pandemic, and they imagined me, a newcomer to the village, alone in my house, without a car, perishing. I was touched by their concern, and their generosity. But they were in their eighties—and the balance felt off: shouldn't *I* be doing something for them?

I soon came to know that Frances and Jackie are people who will do just about anything for anyone, and, if possible, for everyone. They are the indefatigable forces behind "Glenarm in Bloom"—an initiative to brighten up the village with flower beds and colorful planters, for which they have won awards (Jackie was well known as a talented gardener). They are regulars at the weekly Friendship Club at the village hall, where Glenarm people, mostly the elders, gather on Tuesday afternoons for tea and coffee and cakes and conversation, sometimes presentations on local history, singalongs (or "sing-songs," as they're called here), and games. They are members of the Village Committee. They make sure that Glenarm is decked out with lights at Christmastime— around the harbor, up the Vennel, on Toberwine Street, at the entrance to the forest, and their own house is a holiday light-show spectacular in itself—the closest any house in Glenarm comes to the merry Yuletide madness of Brooklyn's Dyker Heights neighborhood, which I loved to visit.

They have also, as I learned the first time I visited them at home, taken in three rescue cats: a stout brown tiger called Magill, whom I'd often seen padding down Mark Street like he owns it; a homebody tuxedo called Emma; and Flora, a sleek, small, shy black cat who seldom comes down the stairs when company's around. And then there's Trevor, their rescued tortoise, who lumbers around their sitting room in slow, mesmerizing circles, and occasionally lifts up a footstool with his shell like a reptilian Atlas—an impressive feat of strength. But then, I already knew from my own experience that Frances and Jackie were particularly friendly to strays.

They live in the house where Frances was born in 1940, and where she was raised. The entrance to the front patio is flanked by topiaries shaped like giant mushroom caps and hollowed in their centers, and the patio itself overbrims with begonias and geraniums in cheerful yellow and purples. Inside, the house is teeming with objects, but it does not feel cluttered; it is neat and cozy, a well-loved and comfortable space that reflects the style, and tells the story, of the people who live there. In the lounge, landscape paintings line the walls, collections of mechanical toys and mementos fill glass-fronted cupboards, a large blue-and-white area rug tops the brown wall-to-wall carpeting, a bookcase overflows beside a fireplace glowing even on a July day. A collection of clocks sounds the time every hour on the hour, in whistles and rings and cuckoos and dings and dongs. Behind the living room, through glass-paneled French doors, is a smaller room devoted mostly to their collection of Waterford crystal and other treasured keepsakes.

Jackie was born in 1934, about a ten-minute walk down the hill from the house on Mark Street, in a cottage on the grounds of Glenarm Castle, to an Irish Catholic mother, Ethel, and a Protestant gardener, David—the head gardener at the Castle. "He was a Scotsman," Jackie told me, relaxing into storytelling. "And in them days, it was prestigious to have a Scottish gardener. They were written to be the cream of the world." Here, in the greenhouse at Glenarm Castle, way up north (in the 55th parallel, at the same latitude as the Alaskan Panhandle and the northernmost point in Germany—but blessed by the Gulf Stream, which keeps us from ever getting unbearably cold), David Wilson—whom his son Jackie modestly describes as "half-clever as a gardener"—grew melons, bananas, oranges, lemons, pineapples, and other rare and luxurious fruits for Lord and Lady Antrim. There were grapes, too, which Jackie remembers his father trimming late at night into perfect, V-shaped clusters, as they could not appear on the earl's tables any other way.

Jackie was born three months before Alexander Randal Mark McDonnell, who was the Viscount Dunluce until 1977, when his father died and he became the 9th Earl of Antrim. The gardener's son grew up the best of mates with the nobleman, a friendship that endured until the earl's death in 2021. "I couldn't say 'Alexander' when I was a child—so I called him 'Lordy,' and always have."

He laughed, and I did, too—but I wondered if there could have truly been parity between the boys, especially as they grew older. In Jackie's telling, there was. In Frances and Jackie's memory, little division existed at all in the Glenarm of their youth. "What we had is our community," Jackie said—using the word more softly than usual here, without the tinge of suppressed hostility, or euphemism, to which I had grown accustomed.

And, echoing Mona, Frances added: "You didn't have to go anywhere for anything." She and Jackie, too, ran through an inventory of Glenarm's shops and attractions and institutions in their early years for me: the bank and the courthouse, the post office, the hardware shop, the nine or eleven (depending on the year) pubs, the three hotels, the presence of the army and the air force during the Second World War, the cinema, the sweets shops and haberdashers and newsagents. . . .

In his time, and place, Jackie was unusual as an only child. Frances—born a McAllister, like so many others in the village—came from a somewhat larger, more typical family, with two sisters, Bernadette and Kathleen, and another who died in infancy. Just as Jackie couldn't pronounce "Alexander," Bernadette had trouble with the name Kathleen, so she called her sister Cash instead, and the nickname stuck—the whole family called her Cash. Their father, Clement, had a garage in Glenarm with one of his six brothers. Another brother was one of the village's three butchers. Another owned the grocery shop where the Bridge Hall is now, where there was an egg-grading station on the lower level, and where he hung dried fish from hooks outside. "This is what he used to say," Frances told me, "that if the fish was limp there was going to be rain."

Long before I met Frances, I'd heard stories about her sister Bernadette—known by everyone as Bernie, a person who, as far as I can tell, was universally beloved in Glenarm. Ten years older than Frances, Bernie moved to New York—Cash had preceded her there—at age thirty, and settled among other Irish immigrants in Inwood, at the very top of Manhattan island. Working as a waitress in midtown, she often served coffee to executives from the nearby offices of Viacom—the powerful media and entertainment company (which later merged with CBS and is now part of Paramount). One of the executives was so charmed by Bernie, so impressed by her humor and work ethic, that he hired her to be his office's "coffee lady," who served drinks and snacks. She continued to work for Sumner Redstone until she retired at eighty and moved home to Glenarm, where she bought the house next door to the one she grew up in on Mark Street. By then her husband, Jim, an Irishman she had met and married in America, had died.

People in Glenarm get emotional when Bernie's name comes up in conversation; their love for her always shines through. One woman told me that after her husband had a health crisis and struggled to quit smoking, a prayer to St. Anthony from Bernie— "She was a great one for St. Anthony," the woman said—finally did the trick. *A great wee woman. Always ready with a story and a cuppa by the fire. Oh, it's a shame you never met Bernie. You would've had the craic about New York.* I missed my chance by a year. I wish I could've baked some bagels for her, and swapped New York stories around her hearth.

Cash stayed in America for the rest of her life, marrying and raising four children in the Bronx. Bernie, however, always intended to return to Glenarm—someday. And so did Frances: she, too, moved away for many decades, but not nearly as far away.

Frances and Jackie met when she was thirteen and he was nineteen—on the village's tennis courts on the estate side of Glenarm Forest, the courts Mona Hyndman had told me about that no longer exist. Their courtship did not begin immediately, as Frances was so young, but slowly bloomed. When they were a few years older, Jackie's father had a falling-out with his boss, the then Earl of Antrim (Lordy's father), "over French potatoes," Frances said. I thought it might be a local idiom that meant "over nothing"—but it was, literally, over a crop of a French variety of potato.

David took a new gardening job at an estate in County Down, but when Ethel moved there to join him, and was seen going to the Catholic chapel, he was fired.

An offer came from his native Scotland—for a gardening position at the Dochfour Estate in Inverness. Not yet married, Frances and Jackie followed him and Ethel there, across the Irish Sea. "The story obviously was that Frances was pregnant," Jackie said, "village gossip."

But the "obvious story," the whispered one, wasn't the true story, even though Frances and Jackie left Glenarm together a year before they married in 1959, which they knew would generate some controversy. Like so many young people from Ireland's villages, in the north and in the south, the main thing that drew them away was the promise of greater opportunity, of work—which Jackie found quickly in Scotland, as a lorry driver.

Frances looked pensive during this part of our conversation. She mentioned something about difficulties with her family in

Glenarm—"It wasn't marvelous at home"—then dropped it. I was curious to know more, but I didn't press. By the time Frances had left for Inverness, her sister Cash had already moved to America. Bernie stayed in the village until she was thirty, when she joined Cash in New York.

Compared to Glenarm, even at its peak as a thriving, bustling coastal village, Inverness was enormous. As soon as he and Frances got there, Jackie remembers, "We said we're not going to stay. As soon as we get a shilling or two together, we're back to Glenarm."

More than fifty years later, they came home. To stay.

Because of their long history with Glenarm Castle—where Jackie was born—the Wilsons have an intimate and warm relationship with "the estate," as a castle and its grounds are called in this part of the world. If they'd ever had any hard feelings about the French potatoes, they had long since softened. Although Jackie's old friend Lordy wasn't often in residence in the years before his death, his son Randal—it is tradition that the Dunluce men are alternately named Alexander and Randal—was, and Frances and Jackie were on friendly terms with the whole family. Frances is Randal's godmother.

My own perspective on the castle is more distant, and conflicted. That I have benefited from some of its resources, despite my distaste for hierarchy and heraldry, is inarguable: the keys to the Barbican, its gatehouse, were my first keys to Glenarm. Were it not for the Barbican, I might never have even known about the village. I have enjoyed regular walks in the estate's serene, beautifully landscapéd walled gardens, and whenever friends visit from New York and elsewhere, I take them there.

When I first came here, the estate's commercial amenities were limited to the café and a boutique. Since then, it has become an increasingly corporate affair, branded with green-and-white signage, with an electric security gate at the entrance, and with more shops and places to eat: an ice-cream parlor, a "pizza pavilion," and a cute outdoor coffee kiosk. None of these are independent, locally run businesses, even if they were designed to look like they are: they're all overseen by a coffee bar chain based in Coleraine. They do employ local people, from here in the village, but they do not operate, in the main, to serve the people of Glenarm. What use is a pizzeria that operates for about six months a year, and usually closes before six o'clock to a person who works long days and doesn't get home until later?

Since my first time in Glenarm, the estate's "welcome center" has expanded to sell artisanal chocolates and stylish gardening gear; there's now a small museum dedicated to the history of the McDonnell family and a rustic little outdoor theater where musical events are staged in the summer. I appreciate these resources and have availed of all of them. Yet I believe that the castle can, and should, do more for the village with which it shares its name, and for the people of this village. (My antipathy surged when the estate curtailed the membership discount it had previously extended to residents of Glenarm—a gesture that seemed not only ungenerous, but foolish and shortsighted, and which meant that I could no longer afford to walk in the gardens whenever the mood struck.)

Sometimes I do hear others voice critical opinions about the estate, quietly, and not often. But when I spoke with Colin Urwin in 2020, he volunteered that he, too, thinks the estate could do more for Glenarm. "They don't have control over everything, but they're the big players here," he said, referring to the estate's status with regional political bodies, implying—rightly, I think—that they could use their influence to help improve Glenarm, to repair the derelict buildings, to attract more business. "They could have the village's interests at heart." In this, and many other ways, our conversation surprised me.

You might remember Colin: the storyteller I met outside the Glenarm Visitor Centre the day I moved here to live full-time, when I thought I was locked out of my house, when I was stung by a wasp. I thought, as a professional storyteller who specializes in tales from the Glens, he'd be a great source of information on local legends and lore. Since we met, I have seen and heard him at work, and he is a terrific teller of tales. But his skills and experience range widely: now I know that he is also a talented singer and songwriter, who has also worked as a professional falconer, and that, as young man during the height of the Troubles, he was a policeman in Belfast.

"I'm only starting to get comfortable talking about it," he told me. The son of an English Protestant father and an Irish Catholic mother, Colin grew up in Larne, a town twenty minutes down the coast from Glenarm, with a long history of staunch Loyalism; I have heard the expression "keep your head lower than a Larne Catholic"—lie low, very low—in a few variations. The reputation maintains. It is a tradition among Loyalists to have bonfires on July 11—the night before the big marches on the twelfth—and for the past two years, the Larne neighborhood Craigyhill has out-done every other Loyalist enclave in Northern Ireland to erect the biggest bonfires of all. In 2022, it was 202 feet tall—about as high as a twenty-story building. On the bus to and from Belfast, I sometimes watched the huge crane hoisting pallets high into the air, swelling the tower with each release of its metal jaws.

In high school, Colin courted a Glenarm girl, Carol, and they married young. He had wanted to go to university to study lit-erature, but with a family to support, it was out of the question. During the Troubles, Colin says, police work paid a high wage, be-cause it wasn't a job many were willing to take at the time. "You got paid better than a schoolteacher, and as much as a junior doctor." Before he entered the Royal Ulster Constabulary (RUC)—which was renamed the Police Service of Northern Ireland (PSNI) in 2001—he and Carol were living in Larne with their infant daugh-ter, and sectarian violence was rising. When they were burned out of their own house by a petrol bomb, it was time to leave.

He'd fallen in love with Glenarm in high school, when he fell in love with Carol. Glenarm was to him, even then, a respite from Larne—which isn't a huge town, but is much bigger and more suburban in feeling than the village. Like all of us who fall for Glenarm, he was entranced by its natural beauty: "Glenarm just opened up a whole new world of wildlife and nature." But back then, he says, "You couldn't buy a house in Glenarm for love nor money." When one finally came up for sale, he and Carol jumped on the opportunity. "In some way," Colin says, "Glenarm saved my life." And just as Carol had loved her childhood here, it turned out to be an idyllic place to raise their own children, who went to

Seaview, who jumped in the river to swim on summer days, who knew the woods and the fields intimately, who learned to respect and cherish nature and wild creatures as much as their parents did.

Colin's love for Glenarm—and gratitude for it—came through clearly. But he also has a considered critique of the village, just as he does of the estate. We never did get around to talking about folktales and legends, not during that conversation anyway. But our talk was illuminating in ways I hadn't expected. Part of what appealed to me about Glenarm was its demographic balance—its population is as close to half Catholic and half Protestant as you're likely to find in County Antrim, and perhaps even in the country as a whole. I liked that about it: I preferred to visit, and live in, a village not dominated by people of one faith—one community—or another. I told Colin that I see that as a virtue.

"It might not be a virtue in practical terms, as far as getting things done," he said, "but on paper it definitely is a virtue, and most of the time it really works." It's certainly different from the Larne of his childhood, where "for two weeks in the summertime, a few of our Protestant neighbors didn't speak to us. That didn't last for a fortnight in Glenarm, only for a night or two." But while the people of Glenarm are not only civil to one another, but friendly, it doesn't mean that they agree on critical issues, on what the future of the village should look like, on how they vote. "Glenarm is held back in my opinion," Colin said, "by the whole community not being able to come together on big issues."

What happens with Seaview, in its bid to become an officially integrated school, he said, "will really be worth watching."

. . . .

In this case, almost everyone in Glenarm did come together: on September 1, 2021, Seaview made history as the first formerly Catholic school in Northern Ireland to become officially integrated, and opened its doors to students for the first time with its new name: Seaview Integrated Primary School. The school held a competition to design its new logo—everyone in the village was invited to submit a design. The winner came from a family whose own children were Seaview students. Inside a circle, it depicts the Glenarm River and the bridge that crosses it near its meeting with the sea. It takes us farther upriver, to the part that lies in the forest, surrounded by trees. Waves of blues and golds represent the ocean—and the farms. At the bottom of the circle, two hands join.

Community, in its most precious and uncynical form, *does* live here. And because I live here, too, I am part of it. I played the smallest role in the integration process—I went to meetings, I signed petitions, and I wrote letters. But I felt I had at least done something to help the village not only survive, but heal. And I felt that I was healing, too.

8

ONE EVENING IN JANUARY 2020, MY FRIEND JACKY
Geary (the one who'd planted the herbs in my garden before I
arrived in Glenarm—not to be confused with Jackie Wilson, Frances's husband) came over for a glass of wine. I had NPR on in
the background—an old habit I hadn't given up—and we quieted
down to listen to another report from China about the new virus
in the city of Wuhan.

"It'll come here," Jacky said.

"Here here?" I asked. "To Glenarm?"

She nodded yes. There was a sting at the base of my spine, a
sensation I feel whenever I am suddenly made nervous, or feel
threatened. If Jacky thought this virus would find its way even to
our little, faraway village, I believed her.

Jacky is an artist, admired for her fine architectural drawings and
paintings, and her beautiful nature and landscape photographs in
the Glenarm calendar she publishes annually to raise funds for the
village and its wildlife group. But Jacky is also a virologist, who
spent much of her professional life working as an HIV/AIDS researcher. Jacky knows viruses. Long before the rest of us had started

stockpiling hand sanitizer, Jacky always kept a bottle in her coat pocket.

A month later, on February 27, I had just finished a bowl of ramen in a restaurant on Belfast's Ormeau Road when I heard more news on the radio, this time the local BBC station: the virus had arrived in Northern Ireland. I made two more trips to the city from Glenarm after that, and left Belfast on February 16, not knowing that that would be the last time I would see the capital city for exactly one year. I remember waiting for the bus home, outside the fruit-and-veg shop on Bridge Street and what I called Jesus's Own Butcher Shop (all the Bible tracts you could want—free with your chicken fillets or pork chops). I often shopped at both before returning to Glenarm from Belfast. An old man who may not have even known that the virus had landed in Belfast sat too close to me on the bench, and breathed loudly; I stood up and paced. On the bus, a young man sneezed ballistically, three times—*kapow, kapow, kapow*—and I wondered if that had doomed his fellow passengers and our driver. I was relieved to get back to the village, even if I could still hear Jacky's prediction—that coronavirus would come here, too—ringing in my mind.

The bar that Mark managed would stay open through St. Patrick's Day. I was outraged, and worried. We knew so little then, but it seemed like common sense that it would be smart to sit this St. Patrick's Day out, discourage crowds, lie low, and wait to learn more about the virus. All we'd been told was to wash our hands, thoroughly and often. No one had said anything about masks yet. I knew that Mark would be careful, but I had little faith in the sort of customer who might show up in a pub on St. Patrick's Day during what had been declared a pandemic by the World Health Organization one week before.

It turned out to be slow and quiet for St. Patrick's Day in a popular Belfast bar, but not without perils: Mark later told me about the customer who clutched her credit card between her teeth before trying to hand it to him to pay her tab (he wouldn't touch it) and about the sometimes charming but often truculent regular who "joked" about spitting on another patron. Mark was not amused.

Two days later, he cleaned the bar from the floorboards to the rafters, disconnected the kegs, salvaged the perishables, cancelled the deliveries, and boarded up the windows. And on Friday, March 20, he came to Glenarm to lock down with me; for how long, we didn't know. His hands were scuffed and pink from all the scrubbing, from all the sanitizing spray he aimed at the bar, the bottles, the stools, the till, and himself. Concerned that he might have contracted the virus in his final days behind the bar, for two weeks we slept in separate rooms, used separate toilets, and sat at opposite ends of the table, like a cartoon king and queen, with the dining room window opened wide.

Among the few possessions Mark brought with him were two worn but sturdy old books he'd had since he was in his twenties, when he was in college in Liverpool, studying ecology. One was a thick paperback for the identification of mushrooms and other fungi, the other a heavy hardback, *The Complete Birdwatcher's Illustrated Guide*. I loved that these were the books he cared enough about to gather and pack quickly, like the only treasures essential and life-sustaining enough to pluck from a burning house. He stationed the bird guide on the kitchen counter, beside the window, next to the few cookbooks I had, within reach of the binoculars he'd given me the previous Christmas—"A gift for the house," he'd said, making me raise my eyebrows and say, "I think you mean, a gift for *you*."

It was mid-April, one month into our first lockdown, when I watched Mark pull a plastic Lucozade bottle from the recycling bin and wondered, as I often do, *What is he up to now?*

He washed it. He drilled a few holes in its trunk. Then he stuck twigs into some of those holes, for perches, and knotted a length of twine around its neck.

Mark scavenges. Mark forages. Mark reuses, reimagines, recycles, upcycles. Mark has learned from his grandmothers to waste nothing. He is a tireless maker of things, things almost always fashioned from found objects and other castoff bits. In late March, having seen me despair of the spice-jar chaos in our cupboards, he put together a spice rack from part of the wooden board that came with the Serrano ham his youngest sister had given us for Christmas and a disassembled wooden fruit crate (he even reused its staples—there were no nails or tools in the house then). The Lucozade-bottle bird feeder was the second of the many things he would make for us, our house, our yard, our garden—and the animals who lived among us.

I checked several wildlife websites to make sure muesli wasn't harmful to garden birds, and Mark filled the bottle and hung it from our laundry line. And so it was that what had been the least romantic object imaginable—a plastic vessel that once held five

hundred milliliters of biohazard-orange-colored sugar-water—
heralded the beginning of one of my life's great loves, and would
also deepen a romance that had long since begun, but which was,
during that strange and uncertain time, slowly blooming in the
dark, stony soil of the Glens.

Mark grew up in the small city of Armagh, about forty miles
southwest of Belfast, close to the border with the Republic of
Ireland, not in the countryside—but I have come to know that he
is, at heart, a nature boy. I had not known that when we met in
2010, but his love for nature, for plants and rocks and birds and
bugs and bats, began to reveal itself when we first stayed in Glenarm in 2016 and took a long walk in the forest together, so long
that we wandered off the trail without even knowing it, and had
logged more than seven miles by the time we went through the
gates and reentered the village, thirsty, achy, exhausted, and exhil-
arated. A few years later, when we toured the botanical gardens
in Oaxaca on a trip there together in 2019, I was impressed when
he was always the first to answer, correctly, our knowledgeable
botanist guide's questions about plants and soil and climate and
ecological processes.

Any concerns I had that he, who had lived in Belfast for nearly
twenty years—who loved its pubs and people and craic and
thrum, who seemed to know and be known by almost everyone we bumped into in the narrow streets of the city's Cathedral
Quarter—might not take to rural living were quelled: he spent
more hours combing the beach than I did, gathering driftwood

and shells and sea glass and, after I'd told him what they were, he also looked for hag stones: rocks with naturally formed holes running through them. I'd been given two such stones by a friend in New York years earlier, who'd collected them on a beach in Kent, and they joined my small hoard of talismans. I loved the look of them, and the name of them—if I ever pull together the spooky folk-rock revival band of my dreams, it will be called Hagstone— and the lore of them: protectors of sailors, guardians of chickens, safeguards against nightmares if hung from a bedpost, also known as adder stones (it was believed by some that adders had bored the holes through them), witch stones, snake's eggs, and Druids' glass. The Scarborough Museum in England has a collection, including ones "mainly hung in houses or stables to keep out witches," and two from right here in County Antrim "that were hung on the horns of cows to prevent fairies stealing the milk."

Hag stones, Mark agrees, are good things. He has collected nearly a dozen of them now, the best of which are part of the motley tableau I've arranged on our mantel, along with Glenarm seashells, family photos, a small, carved wooden hand I brought with me from New York, a drawing of a lamb with the face of William Blake that a friend made for me as a farewell gift, and, now, too, a life-size felted robin with spindly wire legs, made by a German woman named Sonja who lives nearby. When I saw her felted robin at one of the few village crafts fairs that was permitted during the summer, I had to have it: and now, more than any of these other precious objects on the mantel, the robin is the one that reminds me that this is home.

. . . .

It wasn't long before a plump robin alit on one of the perches on the Lucozade bottle, and took his or her (even robin experts say it's hard to tell) fill of cereal. And soon another robin joined in—a scrawnier bird, the red markings on its bony breast so strikingly jagged that the overall effect reminded me of a Clyfford Still painting. Mark named the scraggly one Stan, the plump one Ollie. And the sight of these little creatures, with their orange-red bibs and skinny legs, their habit of jerkily bobbing their stiff tail feathers up and then down, their endearing way of cocking the head in one direction and then the other, supplied a sensation about which I'd long since grown suspicious.

Wonder!

I'd heard quite enough about wonder and its flashy, show-off cousin, astonishment. They turned up in too many poems, too many books and blurbs, too many essays and articles. *Wonder! Astonishment!* If everyone was going around rapt with wonder and wide-eyed with astonishment all the time, what could these things even mean?

Could wonder be sought out—or did it have to come, unbidden, so that one might be, like Wordsworth, surprised by joy? I'd never been sure, but in the years since Frank died, my position hardened. If wonder, real wonder, were to come my way, it would have to be big, extraordinary, not the smallish stuff of everyday life. The way people used the word, it seemed awfully close to whimsy, and whimsy makes me cringe.

Even worse: *childlike wonder!* This notion—this thing we are supposed to have dropped somewhere on the road to adulthood, and which we are urged to try to rediscover and rekindle—that certain experiences, certain sights, certain feelings fill children with rapturous amazement: I didn't really buy it. Maybe sometimes? I don't know. I think back on my childhood and search for instances of wonder and not much comes up. Childhood fear. Childhood worry. Childhood shame. All those were easy to summon. But not wonder. There is a photograph of me at age four or five, when my family was on vacation in Colonial Williamsburg. I am wearing an old-fashioned bonnet and smiling from ear to ear—because my brother, opposite me, was locked up in ye olde stocks, and I was thrilled by his confinement. Was that my idea of childhood wonder? Maybe I was just wonder-deficient. Maybe I was the problem.

Wonder!

Not only had I become leery of it, but some part of me had even come to resent it, if one can resent something one isn't convinced exists. When was the last time I had felt it—or had let myself feel it—anyway? I had to think about that.

There had been something like it on one of my last bus rides down the coast to Larne during a wild storm in January, when I watched the highest, most ferocious waves I'd seen on the Irish Sea breach the seawalls and coastline, their huge, heavy spray as solid as it was liquid, lashing the road like a cracking whip, shaking the bus as it worked the tight curves on the Coast Road. I thought of Hokusai's nineteenth-century woodblock print *Under the Wave off Kanagawa*, which, when I saw it in an exhibition at the Metropolitan Museum of Art in 2015, showed me the sublime and terrible fullness of it, which hadn't registered from the many reproductions I'd seen in offices and dorm rooms.

I had, I suppose, conflated the sublime with the wonderful, and had come to expect from the latter the enormity, and the invigorating terror, I received from the former. *The Wave off Kanagawa . . . Mont Blanc . . . Turner's storm-wracked waters . . . Friedrich's wanderer . . .* These were sublime—vast and unknowable. And now, something wonderful had landed in my backyard. Here was wonder, about twenty grams of it, pecking through a hole in a plastic bottle: a cheerful, cheering, tiny thing, whose ability to charm outweighed its small form by magnitudes. Mark and I watched it, together, until it flew away minutes later. No visitor could have pleased us more.

But we understood that even if the Lucozade bottle had drawn Stan and Ollie to us, they deserved better. Mark disappeared for hours each day into the workshop he'd made of a guest room. With some of the driftwood he'd culled from the beach, he crafted a birdhouse—an enchanting and enchanted structure, both rustic and cleverly engineered, with three levels of "rooms" in which birds might shelter and feed. It brought to my mind the hut of the Baba Yaga—the fearsome witch of Slavic folklore—even if it did not stand on chicken legs as hers did. We asked Jacky—who feeds birds and squirrels and hedgehogs in her wooded garden—if she might add a bag of birdseed for us to her next order from the garden center in Larne, which she was happy to do. Now that the birds had a better, more fitting home in our garden, they also should have the right food.

The robins liked the new house, and the new seed mix. So did a great host of house sparrows, a chime of wrens, a bevy (or *piteousness*!) of collared doves, a clattering of jackdaws, plenty of tits—blue, coal, gray—whose name, yes, I know, is hilarious, at least to Americans, and for which I can find no vibrant collective noun, which is probably for the best, and the occasional shy, gorgeous bullfinch with its salmon-pink belly. I named one of the doves Doris—a slow, spacy, sweet-faced bird with a lumbering gait. Mark called the smallest and fastest of the great tits Crazy Tit, but it might as well have named itself, as it was a tit, a crazy one, who dive-bombed the herb planters and swooshed and swooped into the birdhouse at full speed like a fighter pilot. There was also an enormous and charismatic bumblebee I called Bubba, who got drowsily drunk every afternoon off the nectar of the flowering Japanese andromeda in our yard.

This is how we spent most of April and May: we lingered in the garden, we named the birds, and sometimes even the bugs. I planted things and prayed for their growth. Perhaps this is why springtime—COVID springtime, the worst springtime—not only felt charmed to us, but almost, in its many delights and discoveries, prelapsarian. I often thought about an anecdote I'd heard about William Blake and his wife, Catherine. Their friend, and Blake's patron, Thomas Butts turned up at their garden in Lambeth one day, and was aghast to find the couple naked in their summerhouse, reading parts of *Paradise Lost* aloud to each other. Seeing Butts's horror, Blake is said to have cried out, "Come in! It's only Adam and Eve, you know!" Although Mark and I kept our clothes on in the backyard (nudism wouldn't go over well in the conservative, modest Glens), I felt a kind of refreshed innocence, and that maybe, in our very bare-bones garden, in our calm and lovely village, we had found our own portion of paradise.

There was also Edgar the jackdaw, and Joni the blue tit, named, with utmost reverence, for Joni Mitchell. And of course there was Ollie the robin, the first bird we saw at the Lucozade bottle; he, or she, remained, for a time, a regular visitor. But it was Stan—small, skinny, scrappy Stan—who would claim the crown as the king of our garden, and of our hearts.

There was no rain—unheard of! no rain! in Northern Ireland!—for more than a month, from right after St. Patrick's Day to late April, making it the sunniest April on record in Great Britain and Ireland, in a spring so unusually warm and so bright, it felt like a counterweight to the isolated drudgery of life during a pandemic, almost recompense, an unspoken bargain struck to make the sadness and fear and worry bearable. Through that spring, and the rainy Irish summer that followed, Stan became our favorite visitor (other than Jacky, who came by now and then for a glass of wine or cup of tea in the backyard).

Stan was not Christmas-card perfect like Ollie, but he was more sociable, more generous with his time and his presence. And in his presence, I felt like my childhood heroine Mary Lennox, in *The Secret Garden*—the book that made a reader of me, the book that mattered and spoke to me most during the unhappiest times in my childhood, a book I still reread, often—flattered by the bird's attentions, deeply longing to be liked by him. Yes, *there* was something in my childhood that filled me with wonder. That book, that beautiful, hopeful, encouraging book, that I read over and over until the thick glossy pages in my richly illustrated, hardback edition frayed and fell out.

I admired Mary Lennox for her determination, and for her mutability, for her transformation from a sour, imperious little wretch to a giving, no-nonsense nurturer both of people (her cousin Colin) and of plants. And I adored her friend Dickon, the kind, irrepressibly cheery Yorkshire lad who communes with the local animals and seems to know everything there is to know about all growing things—well, he was my first crush.

It was the robin who showed Mary the way into the garden. And when Dickon first sees the robin with her, he knows that the bird has taken a liking to her.

"Aye, he's a friend o' yours," chuckled Dickon.

"Do you really think he is?" cried Mary eagerly. She did so want to know. "Do you really think he likes me?"

"He wouldn't come near thee if he didn't," answered Dickon.

Stan came near me, very near. As I took my own tentative first steps as a gardener that spring, he was my close companion, watching over me as I sowed seeds for lettuces and radishes and spinach, for red kale and Chinese broccoli, always with my *Gardeners' World* beginner's guide to growing vegetables at hand. I wanted Stan to come even closer. I wanted to *know* that Stan liked me. By then, I was a follower of loads of robin-interest accounts on Instagram, and had joined Facebook groups for robin enthusiasts—such as "Robin: The UK'S Favourite Bird." I scrolled through dozens of robin photographs every morning, and envied these fellow robin lovers who could take such up-close, personal portraits, in whose palms the birds nestled and fed, on whose rakes and knees and picnic tables the birds landed and rested—but persisted in the hope that, one day, I would be one of them—an intimate and most favored friend of robins, just like Dickon and Mary. I made donations to the Royal Society for the Protection of Birds. I ordered a big tub of dried mealworms, which I softened with lukewarm water for maximum robin appeal, then set them in a small dish on the sill outside my kitchen window, a feast, I'd read, no robin could resist.

Stan? Do you like me? Please, come closer.

Stan often had the appearance of one on the morning after a hell of a night out, who'd drunk a shot too many and wound up in a bar brawl. Always slightly disheveled, his feathers never quite in place. And always busy, resourceful, determined. He was up to something. Now that we seldom saw Ollie anymore, I wondered if Ollie was indeed a she, and if Stan was her partner, gathering food and other comforts for her nest.

Small, scrappy, busy Stan. A proper Irishman, my *spideog* (the Irish for "robin").

He reminded me of someone.

"You know what I think?" I asked Mark, as we watched Stan through the window. "I think Stan's like you. In bird form."

Mark hadn't noticed the resemblance, but he laughed—and didn't deny the likeness. He knew that I meant it as a compliment. But there was also a truth we could not overlook, a way in which Stan was not like Mark at all: Stan was a bully. Stan was a brawler.

We saw him force wrens and sparrows out of the birdhouse on many occasions, no matter if they were bigger, no matter that he was always outnumbered. He was the boss, and those other birds had to deal with it. Only the jackdaws—those strong, sturdy, shiny corvids, whom I found terrifically handsome, and Mark disliked for their destructiveness—paid him no mind. Even the collared doves, easily thrice his size, but docile of disposition, scattered when he approached. But although Stan may have

embodied these dominant, even belligerent, qualities more no-
ticeably, more boldly, than other robins, they were nonetheless all
pure expressions of robin nature. These little beauties, the darlings
of Christmas cards and wrapping paper, paintings and poems—
are notorious assholes. Or, maybe, if one is willing to look at it
another way, they're survivors.

For all his belligerence to other birds, Stan had become friend
to Mark and me, our master of ceremonies, the flitting, flying,
chirruping point around which our daily lives slowly and gently
rotated; when he greeted us each morning, it was a sign that the
day had begun, that whatever pain and suffering raged in the
world, at least some small thing was right in our corner of it, on
our little patch.

He kept coming closer to me, closer and closer, but never as
close as I wanted. I'd leave mealworms on the ledge just outside
the kitchen window each morning, so that we could have some
time together while I made my coffee. I swear he was flirting with
me. Almost teasing me. He would give something, but he would
not give me everything. And still, I adored him.

I should have been walking. I should have been reading. I
should have been writing. Instead, I stood for hours at the big
kitchen window—our wide-screen bird-viewing station—or sat
in the backyard, hoping to glimpse a robin or two. Hoping that
Stan would at last alight on my knee or shoulder, and that I would
receive from that action a kind of communion, or at least a bene-
diction. Hoping, like Mary Lennox, that a robin would show me
and grace me with its favor, and that I would know it, for certain.

No, no, no: that's wrong. There was nothing else I should have
been doing. Waiting, there in the garden, or there by the window,

to see Stan, and to receive his accidental but thrilling gifts was occupation enough, at least for a time, an awful and uncertain time during which I was strangely, guiltily happy. Even if the virus would get to Glenarm someday, for now I felt safe, in this remote, beautiful village by the sea. And I was in love: with a bird. And with a man. When Frank died, I doubted I'd ever be in a meaning-ful romantic relationship again, and I didn't think I deserved to. Now, I thought that if the virus came for me, it would come after I'd let my guard down and opened my heart again, and had seen that love—and even wonder—were still possible, even for me.

Late in her life, when she was a good deal older than I am now, but some years before the beginning of her end, my mother be-came a bird lover.

One of the last gifts I remember her talking about, with real excitement, was the Audubon Society's illustrated *Sibley Guide to Birds*, given to her by my brother. My mother gave gifts joyfully, generously, and entirely beyond her means, and expected the same of those who gave gifts to her. My mother, who had made outra-geous demands for gifts from her own adolescent children, things we couldn't possibly afford—a Vuitton bag! A Missoni hat!—was thrilled by the gift of a guide to birds. What had happened? I wasn't sure—but I liked it.

She had always loved animals, had always taken in strays. I have sometimes told myself that she liked animals much more than she liked people, but I am no longer sure that this is true. Certainly, she loved them without the expectations, usually disappointed, that she imposed on humans, without the conditions and demands she made of us. For a few years, she lived in a two-bedroom Manhattan apartment with two dogs, six cats, and a parrot.

The parrot had entered our lives, by surprise, many years earlier, when I was eleven or twelve and we lived where Horatio Street ends at the Hudson River, in Manhattan's meatpacking district, when it was still a place where cow carcasses lay splayed and bloody on the cobbled streets in the early morning after they had been stripped almost clean, where prostitutes worked the street corners, where ours was one of the few families with children in our large building, which took up most of a city block and had been the first of what would be many former meat-processing plants to be converted into residential lofts. Our neighbors were mostly middle-aged single people and couples, and many of them were gay men.

We'd grown close to one couple on our floor, who became the creative, adventurous, insanely fun surrogate uncles of my dreams, who gave me gifts of vintage jewelry and books. Together, they'd written a big, juicy romance novel under a pen name; it was a hit, and when it was made into a television miniseries, they'd struck gold. They filled their triplex with art and important furniture. They bought a pair of shiny red-and-black motorcycles. And they got a parrot—a medium-size, mostly green conure not quite as tall as a Barbie doll, with apple-red cheeks, a severe, sharp, beige beak, rings around its eyes as white as Liquid Paper, and just the slightest endearing protrusion of potbelly—whom my mother suspected was, like the paintings and the masks and the uncomfortable chrome chaise longue, mainly a decorative consideration. She was not wrong. Our friends soon tired, even despaired, of the bird, its tuneless racket, and its tiresome living-thing requirements that it be fed, kept clean, and maybe, also, loved.

The day soon arrived: my mother and I returned from grocery shopping to discover the animal, in its cage, on the mat in front of our apartment door. A note was taped to the cage: "Take this bird or we're gonna cook it."

My mother took the bird.

Our only cat at the time was a Himalayan who'd been declawed (a condition for which my mother later felt guilty, and rightly so)—an aging, glamorous, indolent dandy with velvety dark-chocolate boots for paws that gave way to the great puff of creamy, pale gray fur that made up the rest of him. He found the parrot revolting, undignified, loud, and aggressive—and she proved to be all of that, with some redeeming qualities, too—but took no interest in chasing, attacking, or eating her. But our little socio-pathic fuckup of a dog, a shih tzu who seemed to have a surfeit of teeth in his small, frequently foaming mouth, and somehow both an underbite and an overbite, and who had sent every single member of the family to the emergency room at least once, fell madly in love with the parrot. Together, they'd stroll the long nar-row hallway of our apartment side by side, bird to dog, shoulder to shoulder, as though they were quietly and very seriously dis-cussing Plato en route to an ethics seminar.

No one in our family had ever asked for a parrot, no one had ever wanted one—but Judy became part of our lives. We never exactly thought of her as a *bird*. She sparked no interest in us to learn anything more about flying, feathered creatures. She was just another eccentric Schaap, very much one of us—whose disposi-tion bore some resemblance to my mother's: she could be gentle and amusing and affectionate, then quickly turn angry and violent. She held grudges and seldom forgave anyone once her trust had been betrayed: after the dog, her longtime best friend, had a sudden, shocking go at her top feathers, she would have nothing to do with him, not again, not ever. And after I left home, she attacked me whenever I visited (how dare I have left her?), gripping tufts of my hair in her beak and digging her talons into my scalp. But even when I no longer found her charming, I could not relinquish my feelings for her—which remained warm, and caring, even as she scared the shit out of me.

My mother, who drank her coffee from an enormous ceramic beer stein, from which she sipped throughout the day, long after the liquid had gone cold, didn't mind when Judy perched on the edge of the vessel and sipped from it, too. When Judy died, somewhere around the age of fifteen (a long life, though not so long as her species' average life expectancy), my mother felt guilty and blamed herself and her liberal use of commercial cleaning products; she seemed convinced that too much Windex, too much Pledge, too much Fantastik was what had done Judy in. I suspected it wasn't that at all, and instead implicated all that coffee the bird had drunk over all those years. How much caffeine can the tiny heart of a ten-inch animal handle?

Dogs came in and out of our lives, as did many cats. But Judy was our only bird. When she was gone, my mother never considered filling that empty space with another parrot, the way a new dog or cat would usually appear in our home not long after one had died. So I never expected my mother, in her sixties, to become besotted with birds. By then, she was living in a town house beside the Delaware River in a small New Jersey town. She had started feeding the ducks and geese—to the annoyance of neighbors who thought this strange woman of whom they were already suspicious, whose boldness and bad language and colorful clothes already upset their suburban idyll, had further transgressed by encouraging bad behavior in the birds, who were shitting on their lawns. My mother didn't care who she or the animals annoyed, so long as the ducks and geese were happy and fat. Before long, her interest in birds had grown to include cardinals and bluebirds and sparrows—and that, I think, is when my brother gave her the Sibley book.

That my mother, whose life was for so long a tangle of illness and anxiety, found a respite in birds, and pleasure in their beauty and their song, I knew—but I never stopped to think much about *why*, and I never bothered to ask her.

I started to understand it that spring, when birds had become the main thing that got me up in the morning, bringers of, and reasons for, delight in a time that had ripped away so much other joy. This would have pleased my ma, I thought, who had also found, unexpectedly, so much comfort and peace in watching, feeding, and listening to birds.

Early one morning in June, I saw a strange, sweet sight from the kitchen window. There was Stan, on the garden wall, feeding a fledgling. He made several trips to the birdhouse for seed, and then passed the seeds on to the tiny, new bird, beak to beak.

Maybe that meant that his work in our backyard was done.

Not long after, Stan was gone.

He was not on my windowsill, even when I'd left mealworms there for him. He was not in the birdhouses. Not on the fence, or the wall, or the back of a garden chair. Other robins came around, different robins, all beauties, but they were not the one who showed me the way, the one whose presence I waited and longed for every day like I might have longed for and awaited phone calls from a lover, long ago.

Where had he gone off to, that funny bird, my little love, that sign of life?

I imagined him with a tiny canvas rucksack strapped to his back with a bit of twine, hopping the next freight train to the next town to the next humans whose hearts he would fill, then break. That thought was easier to bear than the possibility that he'd run afoul of one of the stray cats that roam the backyards of the village. Or that maybe he had just naturally come to the end of his life; a robin's life span is, on average, about two years (though many live longer—much longer—if they make it through those first two years). That he had spent nearly a quarter of that time with us, and had given us so much, was more than generous. In return, we had tried to be generous with him, too. If Stan had just gone off to spread joy elsewhere, I could accept that, even if I missed him. Mark is sure he saw him return, once or twice, after his abrupt departure. I'm not convinced. I think, perhaps, that we have seen some of Stan's offspring.

I'd never known a creature who lived with such fullness, who embodied the life force, the way Stan had. With every sighting of him, I too felt more alive, more secure, more connected to the world beyond my own anxieties and achings and grief. It interested me, then, that in Ireland the robin is deeply connected to death. I read story after story about those who consider a visit from a robin a visit, too, from a departed loved one—or a sign that that loved one is still with them, still present, still watchful, still looking over them with care. On my online robin forums, I read a post from a woman who'd lost her son too young, but felt that he still was with her in her garden, in the form of a robin. She asked for support; she knew that what she felt was true, but also wanted to be believed. *Do you believe me?* she asked. I answered that I did—and so did many others.

Could Stan possibly be my mother, whose pain had been eased by the birds in her backyard? Was Stan Frank—who cocked his head in just the same, endearing way when he was thinking of how to answer a question? I didn't think so, but the more I read about robins and death, the more I thought that perhaps Stan had been more important to my long process of grief than I'd considered when he was a still a regular visitor, that he was helping to show me the way to a life in which I might coexist both with those I had lost and those, like Mark, who had come later.

When I looked for more stories of robins in Ireland, many were accounts, passed down through oral history, of how the robin got its red breast—by staying by Jesus's side when he was on the cross and absorbing some of his holy blood. This story is told all over Ireland. I also read many cautionary, local tales about the dangers of harming a robin: there was the mean old man who cut one's head off and woke up bald the next day. He deserved worse than that, I thought. Who would dare harm a robin redbreast?

In a tender column in the *Irish Times*, the writer Fiona Gartland recounts many robin stories. In Irish folklore, "to kill a robin was bad luck that would result in a permanent tremor in the offender's hand," and in parts of the country, "if the *spideog* entered the house, it signaled the death of someone in the family." The birds, she writes, "were accepted as messengers for those in the spirit world. Many people still believe that." And she shares her own story, of seeing a robin in her garden only weeks after her father's death, and blessing the bird. "Grief," Gartland concludes, "ebbs and flows, and we take comfort wherever we can find it. I am grateful for the comfort of robins."

I am grateful for that comfort, too. And I am grateful to robins for more than comfort, for more than solace through the first pandemic season, for even more than giving me a connection to my mother that is only joyful, not sad, not painful. I am grateful for the way robins, and the other birds we've come to know, brought Mark and me closer together—gave us something to tend to, together, to observe closely, together, to learn about, together.

I never thought of myself as cynical—only as pessimistic, which seems somehow gentler, less definitive, and, perhaps, an entirely reasonable response to experience, an acknowledgment that terrible things happen, often for no reason at all, and they might as well happen to me as to anyone else. But I think I'd become cynical, too, without really noticing. How else could I have come to be so dismissive of wonder, so disbelieving?

Wonder is real. It exists. I don't feel corny writing out the word anymore. It feels good. Thank you, Stan, for showing the way.

9

I FIRST MET JACKY GEARY IN SUE'S YOGA CLASS AT Seaview Primary School in 2017. She unrolled her mat not far from mine and said hello, in her deep, rich voice, with the most subtle accent of West Yorkshire, where she grew up—so subtle I never would have correctly guessed where she was from. She was dressed in a blue-and-white-striped shirt, reminiscent of those worn by French sailors—or at least what I thought of when I thought about French sailors—and a kerchief loosely knotted around her neck. With her high cheekbones, her closely cropped hair, and that voice, she reminded me of Annie Lennox, if Annie Lennox were a countrywoman.

I don't remember when Jacky first told me that she was a widow, or how it had come up, but when she did, our connection drew closer, at least for me. I had already intuited, in yoga classes, and in the post-yoga drinking sessions at Stevey's pub, that we would be friends. And when she talked about her husband, Pete, who, like Frank, had died of cancer too young, I sensed that ours would be an important friendship, fulfilling my belief that there were things

I could only talk about, freely and without fear, with another early widow.

Does any word weigh more than "widow"? A conversation with Jacky, who is, like me, an "early widow"—she was forty-five when Pete died—prompted the question. "It's a *hard* word," she said, "even the way it's written." I knew what she meant, even though the sound of it is only a whisper cracked by a thudding, heavy *d* even though I'd never thought about it before. The *w* at both ends—like fence posts with sharp, pointy finials. Fences meant to keep things out, that keep other people out.

Ireland *is* better at death and bereavement than many places are. But widows—especially young ones—always stand out, any-where. I think of the great Irish short story writer Mary Lavin, an early widow herself, as the bard of widowhood. In stories like "Happiness," "Memory," "In a Café," and what many consider her masterpiece, "In the Middle of the Fields," widows are centered in familiar scenarios that are no less rich in detail and emotional perception for their depictions of the everyday lives of widows—closely attuned to their protagonists' anxieties and uncertainties, the complexity of their grief, and the isolation and strangeness created by the condition of widowhood.

In his introduction to a 2016 edition of Lavin's collection *In the Middle of the Fields*, Colm Tóibín, whose mother—like the main character in his novel *Nora Webster*—was an early widow, calls its title story "one of the best stories ever written about grief and its aftermath," and notes that in it, the "newly widowed woman has to remake the rules for herself, including the most ordinary rules of behavior."

I'm familiar with the challenge Lavin depicts and Tóibín describes, and suspect that all other widows are, too. And in addition to this internal pressure, to the rules newly widowed women have to remake, there are (as both Lavin and Tóibín address in their fiction) external pressures, too—pressures of social status, of economics, and of received perception.

In her essay "Mary Lavin and Writing Women," the author Mary Gordon writes:

> A widow is by definition a marginal creature—vulnerable, inaccessible, and yet calling up suggestions of unasked-for responsibility on the part of the more fortunate: as in widows and orphans. She is in need of protection and she can only earn that protection if her reputation is spotless.

For as long as I have worn the label "widow" myself, I have felt that it imposes an extra coat of tragedy on something that is already unhappy enough.

Not so long ago in Ireland, a woman whose husband preceded her in death might have been called a "widow-woman"—a casual bit of everyday speech that nonetheless says something not so casual. *Widow-woman*, as though to be a widow is to be something that is not a woman, but a woman in need of, if not a living spouse, a qualifier, a modifier, a descriptor. It is occupational in effect—cleaning woman, policewoman, widow-woman—as though widowhood is a job, and it sometimes does feel like one.

In *English as We Speak It in Ireland*, first published in 1910, the historian Patrick Weston Joyce wrote: "Widow-woman and widow-man are used for *widow* and *widower*, especially in Ulster:

but *widow-woman* is heard everywhere." My friend Brigid remembers hearing the phrase when she was growing up in Belfast's Ardoyne neighborhood in the 1960s. In the digital archives of the Irish National Folklore Collection (dúchas.ie, perhaps the most rewarding online rabbit hole I've ever jumped into) there are 144 tales featuring widow-women collected in twenty-one of the twenty-six counties in the Republic of Ireland.

In many of these stories the widow-woman is an object of pity. In others, she is of some practical use: "To cure ringworm. Find an old widow woman not related to sufferer. Rub her gold ring on affected part," goes an entry in a long list of traditional cures from County Kildare. Some poignant tales come from the 1840s, the time of the Great Famine, during which almost one million Irish people died and more left the country; in one, a widow-woman has lost eleven of her twelve sons to starvation, and by a single stroke of good fortune, finds thirty shillings while running her fingers through sand—enough money to buy a meal to save her only remaining child. (How many widows were made by the famine? How many wives left behind in the waves of emigration that followed?)

Another story begins with the line, "There was an old woman living with herself." Whether the teller of the tale intended this or not, *with* herself hits harder, and truer, than *by* herself: as a widow, I have sometimes felt the doubleness it suggests, that I am both myself and *herself*—woman and widow—and they do not always get along.

Many of the women in these old tales—like the biblical Naomi/Mara—are embittered by their widowhood. Some are witches—the malevolent, cursing kind. In a story from County

THE SLOW ROAD NORTH

Donegal, a widow-woman covertly steals milk from her neighbors' cows by turning herself into a hare. A man in the village catches on to her ruse, and sends his hound after the hare. In the end, the man enters the widow-woman's house, "and found her lying moaning in her bed and her legs all bleeding and torn."

Long before I knew any of these stories, or had read anything by Mary Lavin, before I had read the painful, true accounts of women widowed by the Easter Rising and, later, by the Troubles, before a librarian in Belfast's splendid Linen Hall Library gently rested a copy of *A Lament for Art O'Leary*—an eighteenth-century poem that is the urtext of Irish widowhood, in a beautiful, rare edition with illustrations by Jack B. Yeats—on the desk where I was working. She also told me to read Doireann Ní Ghríofa's extraordinary book, *A Ghost in the Throat*, which is in part an exploration of the poem and its widowed author, Eibhlín Dubh. But there was one widow-woman in Irish literature I had already come to know well: the Widow Quin, the formidable and unforgettable creation of J. M. Synge in his play *The Playboy of the Western World*, perhaps the most famous, and widely staged, of all Irish dramas.

It was scandalous in its time: a tale of (presumed) patricide in the west of Ireland, centered on an act of outlandish violence. Synge also dared to use the word "shift"—meaning, in this case, a women's undergarment—and because of this, there were riots at the play's premiere. Even if the word "shift" now sounds quaint, the play retains the power to shock. And the Widow Quin, as she is called in the dramatis personae and throughout, is inextricable from her circumstances and condition, her widowhood—and is one of the play's most powerful agents of shock. Like the poor Donegal widow-woman who turned into a hare to steal, the Widow Quin is drawn as "a witch woman," as the Northern Irish critic, poet, and novelist Seamus Deane puts it, and "represents the obverse of decency, which is notoriety." She, not Christy Mahon, the protagonist of the play's title, is the "real murderer in the play."

Because early widowhood is seen as unnatural—one spouse will always outlive the other, but not by decades, not so soon—those of us who become widows when we're still too young for the role, are inherently suspect, and notorious, if not for bad deeds we committed, for bad things that happened to those closest and most intimate to us. I remember my first awkward attempts at dating after Frank died, how the word "widow" not only silenced the men I met, but also seemed to spook them—as though my husband's misfortune, and mine, might somehow be contagious. (In contrast, widowers are often seen as desirable, at least in the movies: think of Christopher Plummer's Captain von Trapp in *The Sound of Music*, or Tom Hanks's Sam Baldwin in *Sleepless in Seattle*.) And in my worst moments, when guilt and regret funnel in until they have filled my conscience, I have seen myself as a husband killer.

It was during a trial separation—one that I had asked for, not he—that Frank got cancer. We had agreed, with the mediation of a marriage counselor, to be in touch during our separation only if there was an emergency—with one of us, with anyone in our family, with either of our cats. When the phone rang one afternoon, just as I was about to leave work, as soon as I heard his voice I knew something was wrong. "I have cancer," he said, as plain as that. The next day, he returned to New York. We unseparated, but our marriage had changed. He knew that I had been considering divorce. I knew that divorce wasn't what he wanted. We had been kind and sensitive to each other during our months in counseling—so much so that our counselor praised our civility, our thoughtfulness, our ability to communicate. But: Had I broken his heart? And had his broken heart made a dense and irresolvable knot inside him? Was that knot a tumor? Did it metastasize and kill him? Was I the murderer, then? These thoughts do sound mad. And at times, they did make me feel like I was losing my mind.

The first time I saw *The Playboy of the Western World* was on a low-quality videotape, in an Irish literature class in college, probably in 1992. The last time I saw it, it was a production staged at Belfast's Lyric Theatre in late 2019—the only time Mark and I have gone on a theater date. In this production, the action was updated to sometime in the 1970s and moved to a village near the border between the Republic of Ireland and Northern Ireland, and the Widow Quin was played as a tough, black-leather-jacketed biker chick. I seldom see the point in this kind of updating—as thrilling as the experience was, the futuristic, sci-fi aesthetics of the production of *Das Rheingold* Frank and I saw in Bayreuth were incomprehensible to me—but I admired Aoibhéann McCann's performance as the widow, as attentive to her character's pathos and survival as to her ferocity and ruthlessness.

Of all the plays to see with my first real boyfriend since Frank died, I had to pick *Playboy of the Western World*. Mark hadn't seen it before, and he enjoyed it. I did, too. But, in what still felt like the early days of our romantic relationship—even if had taken nine years to reach that point—one thing he and I had never really talked about was my widowhood. Even in Ireland, where death is discussed openly and often, widowhood is not a topic with which men are comfortable. Part of it, in Mark's case, might be "the famous/Northern reticence" that Seamus Heaney wrote about in his poem "Whatever You Say, Say Nothing." And part of it might also be because his impulse might be the right one: what can a man say about widowhood, a way of living about which he can know nothing? Unless he himself is a "widow-man," and even then, because it is obvious that men and women are treated and seen and understood differently, it is not the same.

If I have found in Northern Ireland a more companionable place to talk about death, to grieve and to live with loss, the very particular feelings engendered by early widowhood are still often hard to talk about, too specific, too personal. There is an exception: it has been easy to talk to other early widows about being one, too.

I have regrets about things I didn't do in the first few years after Frank died that might have helped me. I wish I had taken up his hospice's offer of group bereavement therapy, but every time an envelope arrived with the hospice's logo printed in the top left corner, I tore it up and threw it in the recycling bin just as soon as I'd opened it. I let follow-up calls from hospice volunteers go straight to voicemail, and after a few hours or days I deleted them, unanswered. All of this, I see now, was part of my bid—deliberate or not—to postpone grief, to set it aside for a better time, which I doubted would ever come.

The topography of every new and singular grief is rough and unknown; we who have lost must navigate dark, swollen swamps unseeable on moonless nights, cliffsides too wet too steep too cragged to find a foothold, calm and shallow tributaries that fool us and lead nowhere. But how can we know better, when we are drowning in the muck? In October 2020, many months into the coronavirus pandemic, I attended a weekend-long online event called "Good Grief: A Festival of Love & Loss," and registered for the workshops and webinars that were most attuned to my concerns: "The Healing Power of Nature in Grief," "Delayed Grief," "Grief in Literature," and, perhaps most of all, a session called "Am I Grieving Right?" I looked at all those faces in those little Zoom boxes—looking like "Am I Grieving Right?" might be a game show, during which we'd have to click on buzzers to deliver the right or wrong answer. The chat in the sidebar was busy: most seemed to know, of course, that the answer to the question was there is no right way to grieve. But we still had our nagging hunches, a collective sense of failure or impropriety in the face of a loved one's death.

When I say that I regret how I grieved, I don't quite mean that I did it wrong. What I mean is that I wish, when I had one of those rare flashes of clarity that broke through the murk, I'd have discovered a different way to grieve right. I regret that I hadn't thought to try meeting other early widows, something that could have been arranged by hospice (or probably even on Craigslist). I wish that, even while my mother was dying, I had made time—out of what felt like no time at all—to know other women who were going through their own versions of what I was going through.

But in those years just after Frank died, I neglected all but my oldest, tightest friendships. In most other cases, I turned down invitations, didn't bother to respond to emails and phone calls and letters. If anyone really wanted to see me, I figured, they knew when I worked at the bar—and could come see me there. That took all planning, agency, and effort out of my hands, and put the burden, as it seemed to me then, on them. To build and nurture new friendships when I had let so many old ones languish didn't just seem impossible—really, I hadn't even considered it at all.

In late 2014, I got a Facebook message from a woman I'd met only once, when mutual friends had brought her and her husband to the bar during my shift. I liked the young couple, both journalists, instantly: they were warm and fun and bright. When I read, not two years after that lovely evening, that the husband in the couple had died on a reporting trip at age thirty-nine, I wept. I kept starting to write a condolence card to his wife—his widow— and I could never find the language. And then, after much time had passed, I got her message. She had read an article I'd written about grief—and about how cooking had become one of my better coping mechanisms. She wanted to tell me that it was a relief to find someone else expressing the same feelings she had, and that she related especially closely to one part of it:

> I often shut myself off from nearly everyone who tried
> to help me, and many did. It felt as though no one and
> nothing could help.

I wept again as I read and reread her message, and wrote back to her that day. We made plans to have dinner together not long afterward. She cooked for us at her place—like me, she loves to cook and to feed people, and takes comfort in it. I think it was risotto; whatever it was, it was delicious, and I'd brought plenty of red wine. We talked for hours, about *everything*, but mostly about grief, and trying to cope, and our dead husbands. And it was effortless: I hadn't spoken about any of this with such ease, such a sense of being seen and understood, such unforced compassion. We early widows may be a strange and sad affinity group, but I felt the importance—perhaps even the necessity—of our connection. We met a few more times, but I did not work hard enough to sustain it, and I let us fall out of touch—even though I felt both consoled and buoyed by the presence of another young widow in my life.

When friends in New York asked me, in 2019, why I was moving to Glenarm, I told them I was ready for a significant change, that I wanted to live by the sea and near a forest, that I'd been longing to live in Ireland since 1991, and if I didn't do it now, it was unlikely ever to happen. And I also told them about Jacky, that I'd made a friend in Glenarm—an artist, a scientist, and a widow—and that her friendship was already meaningful to me. Aside from the friend who'd written to me after her own husband died, and whose friendship I didn't try hard enough to maintain, I knew no other widows in my general age group in New York— vast, overstuffed, densely populated New York. But in a tiny village in a part of Ireland that Americans seldom visit, there was someone *like me* in a way that none of my other friends were.

Jacky and I often have coffee together in my backyard in the morning, or a glass of wine or a gin and tonic in the evening. Throughout the pandemic, she was often the only person Mark and I saw regularly—even though she had another small pandemic "bubble" of friends. And if you're only going to socialize with one friend during a pandemic, you could do much worse than a virologist who is also funny, and thoughtful, and game to try whatever weird food you've cooked that week.

After I got here in 2019, when I told Jacky how surprised and comforted I was that she spoke of Pete so openly—and that it gave me more courage to talk about Frank and his life and death—she told me it wasn't always as easy for her as it seemed. "It's still hard to talk about these things," she said, as we sat at my dining table drinking tea on a late-summer afternoon. "I'll talk about aspects of Pete and loss, but not other aspects. I'm quite happy with people telling great, funny stories, remembering things that they and Pete had got up to. And then I'll walk back into the house and wish I could tell Pete about whatever I've just been doing because it would be amusing to him. It's always kind of this mixture—bittersweet. You sort of think, 'I'd love to tell him that. I know he'd laugh'—but you can't." Still, she was willing to sit down with me and talk about Pete, his life, his death, and her life as his wife, his caregiver, and his widow. The contours of our experiences are similar, but there are important differences.

Jacky is as uneasy with the word "widow" as I am—but, in one way, she finds it helpful. When people ask her if she's ever been married, she says yes—and makes it clear that she's widowed. "If they don't know me they assume that I'm divorced, so I always correct them." She doesn't want people to think she "gave Pete up," or that they had a bad marriage. But when people hear the word "widow," she says, "it's a bit awkward and I automatically reassure them that they don't need to be awkward about someone they didn't know." She quickly added that she'd rather they felt awkward about thinking she was divorced, and we both laughed—but of course she wouldn't say that to them. Like me, she finds it easier to talk about widowhood with another widow.

Pete is why Jacky lives in Glenarm: he grew up nearby, on the outskirts of Larne. His father, Tom, was well known throughout the region as a veterinarian, who traveled up and down the glens tending to cows and sheep, dogs and cats—sometimes making his rounds with Pete, the youngest of his three sons. Jacky describes his childhood as very "James Herriot," referring to the beloved British veterinarian and author whose writings inspired the popular television series *All Creatures Great and Small*. "They had a house full of dogs," Jackie said, because whenever anyone, for some selfish reason or other, asked Tom to put their dog down, he wouldn't do it: instead, he took the dog home and made it part of the family. Pete grew up loving all animals—especially dogs.

Dogs brought Pete and Jacky together. At the time, they were both living in Salisbury, England, a place that Jacky describes as "a small city that's really a town," where everybody is bound to meet everybody else sooner or later. Jacky was working at Porton Down, the big, national science research center, and Pete was stationed at a nearby army base. She saw him walking his Rhodesian ridgeback. She had the same kind of dog: she'd fallen in love with the breed when she met a ridgeback on a trip to Africa when she was a young woman, and had vowed then that she would have one of her own someday. (She currently lives with Xsabo, her sixth ridgeback.) Jacky had never been married before—and Pete called her his "favorite wife so far" (she was his third). They were together for six years before they married—and then ten more before he died.

After Pete was diagnosed with aggressive metastatic prostate cancer, Jacky—the scientist—resolved to research his illness and learn everything about it she could; Pete said that whenever he wanted to know something, he would ask her. Her reading was not encouraging: she understood that her husband was, as she put it, "on death row." Jacky already had an intimate acquaintance with profound loss. Her sister, Deborah, had died of cancer two years earlier. Her father died while Pete was ill—from cancer too; when it happened, Jacky and Pete were in Kenya. Long after her first trip to Africa, Jacky had lived in Uganda for two years working as an HIV researcher; Pete had never been anywhere on the continent. They had always wanted to go there together, and decided to make the trip while he was still mobile enough to travel. He had already started feeling pain in his spine—at that point, it was manageable—and they both knew that there would not be another chance for a trip.

Back home in Glenarm, Jacky was Pete's full-time caregiver. Pete didn't want anyone in the village to know about his illness— "He didn't want to become 'the guy with cancer,' and be treated differently"—which Jacky honored, although the secrecy made an already agonizing set of circumstances even harder. But Pete was the one who was dying.

Pete's back pain had worsened. About six months before he died, he and Jacky went to the hospital in Belfast to meet with his oncologist, who told them Pete had to stay there for a ten-day course of radiotherapy. Professor J., as they called him, explained that if they couldn't stop the cancer that was causing the pain from growing, Pete might not be able to walk. He had entered the hospital that day expecting to be home in a few hours, but Professor J. didn't even want Pete to get back in a car—one bump in the road could further harm his damaged spine.

"That was when the downhill slump started," Jacky remembered—and when she started to grieve. "I think that was August, and he died at the end of January. In between, I'd already started mourning, privately, without Pete knowing about it. He didn't want me to be upset about anything." When I asked her what form that mourning had taken, she said, "tremendous sadness." She'd gotten Pete an adjustable, hospital-style bed, so he could change his position depending on where he felt pain. Jacky moved into the small guest bedroom at the back of the house. After Pete had taken his painkillers, they'd have a cup of tea together, and once he had fallen asleep, Jacky would go to the little bedroom; there, she said, "I could do what I liked. If I wanted to cry, he wouldn't know about it. I had a controlled system of only really mourning when I went to bed at night. I didn't want Pete to know that that was going on, and that was really hard."

After his long hospitalization in Belfast, it was no longer possible, in a village as small and neighborly as Glenarm, to keep Pete's illness a secret. By September, he had told some close friends in England, who came to visit for five days. Now that people knew Pete had cancer, and that he was dying, they would tell other people, which was easier for Jacky than sharing the news herself. And with more people coming to visit, bringing meals, helping to keep Pete's spirits up, Jacky could now take an hour off to take their two ridgebacks to the beach.

While Jacky spoke, I listened to her story on its own terms, without comparison to my own. Later, when I thought back on our conversation, the similarities and differences started to take shape. I tried to imagine what it might have felt like to keep Frank's illness secret, and even the imagining filled me with anxiety, an anxiety shaded by pain. But then, I remembered, secrecy was the last thing Frank wanted. From the day he got his diagnosis to the end, he was transparent with everyone—me, our family, his colleagues at the university, and his friends. He wanted everyone to know, and he wanted people around him. He welcomed questions, and answered them honestly and in detail, in his thoughtful, professorial way.

Some of his loved ones found the prospect of visiting him more painful than they thought they could bear—because they knew how serious his prognosis was, because they made agonizing associations with friends who had died, because hospitals are frightening places and they frightened them, for a long list of understandable, human reasons. Knowing how tender and fraught our responses to terminal illnesses can be, knowing how tender and fraught we humans are even in better times, I did not want to put unkind pressure on anyone. But I knew that there was one friend in particular whose company Frank cherished, who always made him laugh, who always sparked conversations, and sometimes debates, about politics and literature. I talked to that friend, and urged him, as gently as I could, to spend some time with Frank. I did not say to him that the desires of the dying are more important than our own, but I believe that. I did not say that if he did not take the opportunity to see Frank now, he would probably never see him again, and that was true, too. I did say that Frank loved him, maybe more than he knew, and that a visit would lift his spirits. Within a week, Paul came around, and both of them were glad that he did.

Frank had to spend his forty-first birthday in a hospital room—and he wanted a party. I asked the staff on his floor if it would be alright to invite a small group of people over to celebrate, and they approved the plan; his December 24 birthday always meant that not everyone he wanted to see would be around and available. But a half dozen close friends came to the hospital that evening, bearing gifts of stinky cheese and luxurious chocolates and champagne. One brought a tiny pink tinsel Christmas tree—a cheering, kitschy, thoughtful gift. Does it sound crazy to say that it was a hell of a party, and that Frank had a fabulous time? It was, and he did.

Just as there is no right or wrong way to grieve, there is no right or wrong way for the dying to behave. Pete wanted privacy. Frank wanted attention. Jacky and I honored their opposite wishes—the needs of the dying outweigh our own, and they require a degree of selflessness for which I never felt equipped. Selflessness is read and perceived as an honor, a distinction, the highest praise; to be called "selfless" is to be regarded as the best and most virtuous thing a person can be. But what a word it is, too. When one strips oneself of selfhood, what can remain? A shell. A cypher. An emptiness. Caregiving is a privilege, and when both Frank and my mother were dying, to not have cared for them would never have crossed my mind. But it is also hard physical, emotional, and practical work.

When Frank died, I was quietly aware of well-known stages of grief like anger, depression, and acceptance, but mostly I felt stagnant. And because my mother was so sick at the time, I had to muster the little energy I had for her. I remember feeling very angry at myself, but not at Frank. That he was removed from this world before his time made me more sad than angry.

Pete died at the end of January. Jacky found loneliness "quite hard to get used to." That June, her mother, who was otherwise in good health, had a serious fall. "She smashed her leg up. Then I was just angry for a while that Pete had died." Her mother's recuperation would be slow. "From the beginning of June to the beginning of September she needed my attention. I was so cross. I was like, 'No, I don't need this yet. I'm not ready to start coping with someone else's ailments'" but it was her mother, whose own husband and elder daughter had died not so long ago, and Jacky wanted to be there for her. Without Pete, she was angry that there was no one to take of *her*.

Taking care is part of the marriage contract: we will be here for one another in sickness and in health. In the end, because one spouse will outlive the other, the contract can only be a one-way deal. And I think that because neither Jacky nor I have children, we share a powerful anxiety about our futures as we get older. Jacky is very close to her neighbor, Nessie, who is approaching her ninetieth birthday—I've observed that there are many long-lived women here in the Glens, and in her case, I attribute her longevity at least in part to the walks she takes every single day. Nessie isn't a widow like Jacky and me, but she is also childless. And I think that's one reason Jacky makes a point of checking in on her often, chatting most days, making sure she's eating. Jacky's cat, Fish, spends almost as much time at Nessie's house as he does at Jacky's, and this arrangement satisfies all parties.

Jacky, the scientist, likens her experience of grief to a sine wave: "Grief actually starts for me before the death, but when the person has died it's all-encompassing. There's a spike in emotions, and as time passes those peaks become less spiky, less high, and the curve becomes shallower, and you've almost come back down to an even keel—even if you're not exactly at the same level you were before the person died." She noticed the pattern, she says, because she repeated it after her sister Debbie's death, then her father's, and then Pete's. I have sometimes wondered if a paradox of the accrual of loss is that it makes each subsequent death a little easier to cope with, but also renders you less and less the person you were before.

It was Pete who brought Jacky to the Glens, and who made a home with her here in Glenarm. After he died, many people in the village asked her if she was going to go home. At first, Jacky felt hurt by the question—did they *want* her to leave? But she realized it was not malicious. It was a reflection of the way many people in Northern Ireland conceive of the idea of what home means. "I don't have the same thing I've noticed a lot of people in Northern Ireland have—this yearning to come back home, and by home I mean their home place, where they were brought up and where most of their family still lives. Whether they live in

Liverpool or Dublin or New Zealand, as the years go by, the bungee cord to Northern Ireland pulls tighter." Pete had that desire to return to the Glens after many years in England—he never thought he'd stay away forever. The same is true of Frances and Jackie Wilson who, even through their many happy decades in Scotland, always knew they'd come home. And for Frances's sister, Bernie, after she'd found success in New York City. I've met many other returnees in the village. Jacky understands why people here feel so strongly about returning, but, she says, "I just never had that concept myself." She grew up in Thornhill in West Yorkshire, which she describes as a lovely village, but neither she nor her parents had been born there. As fond as her childhood memories are, she never considered moving back to Yorkshire.

And she, too, takes solace in Glenarm, especially its seashore—something you won't find in West Yorkshire. It's the closest thing to a home place she's ever had, and she loves it deeply. If an irresistible adventure came up, Jacky would not rule out the possibility of leaving. Still, she says, "I have every intention to die here." The longer I live here, I feel the same way.

10

I AM RUNNING ACROSS A FIELD, AN ENORMOUS field with a top coat of glassy ice, shinier than a crystal ball, slick as rendered goose fat. I'm running toward the woods: there they are, I can see them in the distance, triangles of pine, silvery upright-nesses of birch. The field ends abruptly at the woods' edge, where there stands a small log cabin, lighted by one candle set on the sill of a four-paned window. The cabin can be no larger than one room. It is a homely and endearing sight, and all I want is to get there and to close the door behind me.

Whose cabin was that? Whose woods were those?

It's a dream cabin in dream woods. It exists only in the recur-ring nightmare that besieged me for almost two years, when I was, roughly, between the ages of seven and nine. As an adult, when I have tried to remember the dream in its fullness, the woods have assumed what seems to me a Slavic cast. It's something to do with the way the moon—always a full moon—is veiled by a scrim of slim white birches, by the way the moonlight angles through the narrow gaps between the trees, as if forced by a giant hand. The look of it suggests to me the possibility of happening upon the Baba

Yaga in her hut set high on chicken-leg stilts; she can be a helper and a healer, or a trickster and destroyer. She can be anything. (I imagine her resembling my maternal grandmother, Henrietta, in appearance and disposition—she could be mean, but not to me.)

What do I know about "a Slavic cast"? Grandma Henrietta's parents came from Poland, and other ancestors came from Russia, but I have never even been to either place, and none of that would have mattered to me as a child when I had the dream, and it had me. I wouldn't have known, then, what "Russian" meant, or who the Baba Yaga is. I wouldn't have known what "Irish" meant, either, or who the *sidhe* might be. Time and memory do their work on our childhood dreams, adding and removing, ornamenting and distilling; they pick up a no-name, no-place forest and plonk it down in Russia. But as the locus of fairy tale, of dream, of nightmare, requiring no compass or map to show the way, a forest is always the Forest, the great, universal not-real wood, belonging to no place special and to no one in particular. Real forests are real because they are specific. Back to the dream:

To get to the cabin at the edge of the woods, I must cross that broad, bleak, frozen field. I am still running running running. I am breathing heavily. And somewhere past the halfway mark between where I was running from and where I am running to, I turn to look behind me, and I see only bright animal eyes, dozens of pairs of bright shining animal eyes all fixed on me as though I am nothing more or less than a racetrack rabbit.

My traction fails. I spin and slip on the ice and now I am on my back, and the small of it burns from the fall. I look up and I see that they have caught up with me. They are still nothing but eyes, uncountable flashing eyes, but I know what they are, and I know what wolves want, and I am surrounded. Then I wake up.

Night after night, the dream ended there. I would never know if the wolves attacked me, if they killed me, if they ate me, if I made it to the cabin. But I had the dream, with its ungenerous nonending, hundreds of times, and in my reading of its logic and its rhythms, the only conclusions I could draw, when I thought about it and replayed it as faithfully as I could, and I often did, was that I was a goner. And that I wanted, desperately, to make my way home.

I became so afraid of having the nightmare—which began not long after my parents separated—and of having to witness, some-day, its inevitable end, that I stopped sleeping, because only that could prevent me from having the dream. Instead, I stayed up all night, until the first light came, when nightmares couldn't hap-pen. My sleeplessness made my energy slump and my schoolwork suffer, but none of that was as bad as the dream, as bad as what might happen next if I let it.

I did not want my mother and brother to know that I was not sleeping, that I would not *let myself* sleep. But they knew. How could they not? Our bedrooms were lined up in a row like railroad sleeper cars along the narrow rear corridor of our apartment. It was not a place that lent itself to keeping secrets.

Maybe I should have just said something. My mother, my er-ratic and volatile mother, was, when faced with a medical crisis (insomnia in a child may have qualified) magnificently calm and focused. She, who could hardly subdue her own demons, was in-tuitive and perceptive about the emotional lives of others. She was so good in certain kinds of emergencies, especially cases of extreme physical distress in both people and animals, that I often wondered if she might have been happier and more fulfilled if she had wanted to be a nurse or a doctor or a veterinarian instead of an actress. She never flinched at the sight of blood. Once, when I discovered a huge, engorged tick clamped to our cat's neck, I almost fainted; my mother silently transformed into a field surgeon. She sterilized a pair of tweezers with a match, took cotton pads and antiseptic from a bathroom shelf, and removed the insect. Then she burned it to death.

She didn't try to force me to go to sleep. She did not probe, did not ask about the source of my bedtime terror. She didn't try to blackmail me, and didn't try to bargain. Instead, she gave me sketchpads and pens and pencils, coloring books and notebooks, paperbacks full of puzzles, and book-books, the ones made up mostly of words, too. Among the latter was a small, slim hardback with a blue cover: *Lewis Carroll's Bedside Book: Entertainments for the Wakeful Hours.* It was probably not meant for children, but age-appropriateness was never something my mother concerned herself with. Sometimes this didn't work out: did an eight-year-old whose own parents were going through a mess of a divorce need to sit through *Kramer vs. Kramer*? But sometimes it was *the best.*

Lewis Carroll suffered from insomnia himself, and late in his life, under his given name, Charles Lutwidge Dodgson, the name by which he was known as a mathematician, he published *Pillow-Problems Thought Out During Sleepless Nights.* Some of his seventy-two "pillow-problems" found their way into the *Bedside Book* my mother had given me, which came out in 1979, almost a century after Carroll died. It included short, funny rhymes, and puzzles; I think it even had a few recipes that one might attempt quietly in the kitchen, without any rackety chopping or clanging pots or any of the other noisy things that happen when we cook.

My mother's mostly hands-off approach worked. Given enough quiet late-night activities, with time and without pressure, I became more interested in reading a story, making a sketch, working out a puzzle, than in my nightmare. And when I'd completed enough tasks, when some stimulation or other had knocked me out, I would sleep. There had been stretches, before my insomniac period, when the dream happened every night, for weeks on end, with no break, no respite. Now, when the nightmare came at all, it came only after long intervals without it. Maybe once a month. Then a few times a year. And then—it was gone. But so familiar had we become in our long life together, girl to nightmare, nightmare to girl, that it left its marks impressed on my psyche and, I think, lodged in my sensibilities, where it remains.

Long after the dream had faded, I was still afraid of wolves—even though I'd never seen one up close. Then, in my first or second year at college, an organization called Mission: Wolf, dedicated to giving sanctuary to wolves that people (wrongly!) thought they could keep as pets, came to my campus to teach us about the animals. We sat on the floor of an auditorium, where Mission: Wolf staff members walked a wolf on a long lead inside the circle we had made. I could see why some people thought wolves could be pets: there in the auditorium, the wolf seemed no more threatening than a malamute, just bigger, with massive paws and a cartoon-ishly oversized tongue lolling from its big wet mouth. When the presentation began, I anticipated disaster: this time the wolf *would* try to rip someone's throat out, probably mine.

Instead, it padded around the sprung wooden floor, occasionally stopping to lick a face. A bolt of fear struck my lower spine when one moved toward me—*this was it, this had to be it*—and quickly brushed its big dumb tongue against my cheek; then, nothing. At the end of the evening, I was both relieved and disappointed.

Not long after that encounter, one of my professors gave me a copy of *The Bloody Chamber*, Angela Carter's 1979 collection of reimagined fairy tales, and said, "Read this." Well, he knew what I liked. I loved the ripeness of Carter's lush language, her boldly sexual feminism, and an aphoristic confidence that felt very fresh and wise. In "The Company of Wolves," one of the best and best-known stories in the collection, Carter writes of the character who is her version of Little Red Riding Hood: "she knew the worst wolves are hairy on the inside." And with one suddenly obvious truth, she nearly broke the wolf spell for me.

The following semester, a friend who was well aware of my wolf thing, who mocked it with tender brotherly cruelty, told me about Freud's case of the so-called Wolf Man, who, like me, had a recurring nightmare about wolves. When I checked it out of the library and read it, it was the stillness of the Wolf Man's wolves that gave me the creeps: perfectly, disconcertingly stock-still, seated upright on their haunches, arrayed in the branches of a tree outside a window, motionless. *My* nightmare wolves had been so vigorous, so active, so swift. His were somehow even more menacing, more dreadful.

THE SLOW ROAD NORTH

The worst wolves are hairy on the inside—and perfectly still.
And now, I thought, the spell really was shattered.

If I take a left when I step out my front door, it's just a five-minute
walk to the sea. If I take a right, in five minutes I've got Glenarm
Forest.

I've got. That's not right. The forest does not belong to me. It
was once part of the Glenarm Castle estate, which sits across the
river from it. It is now maintained by the Ulster Wildlife trust,
and is open to all.

When I catch myself sounding like this, possessive of the forest,
I am reminded that I am American, as if I needed reminding of
that. And I sometimes think of that essential American poem by
Robert Frost, "Stopping by Woods on a Snowy Evening," especially its opening stanza—

> *Whose woods these are I think I know.*
> *His house is in the village though;*
> *He will not see me stopping here*
> *To watch his woods fill up with snow.*

—and the destabilizing diction of that first line: "Whose woods
these are I think I know," whose first clause always sounds to my
ears like it wants to be a question—"*Whose woods are these?*"—but
is resisting it, straining against its own inclination.

In the poem's early twentieth-century New England, the woods
would have belonged to *someone*, even if they lacked the "No

Trespassing" and "Private Property" signs now ubiquitous to so much American "wilderness." In the interest of fairness, I am obliged to report that compared to many other parts of the United Kingdom, where the right to roam and ramble, as long as one does not litter or do damage or liberate a farmer's livestock, is held sacred, "private property" is very much a thing here in Northern Ireland, and sometimes fiercely guarded, and there are plenty of places where we who wander would not be welcome. Still, here, I don't have the anxiety I often felt in American woods, whether I saw "No Trespassing" signs staked to trees or just worried that I'd unwittingly wandered onto someone's land, and that that some-one probably had a gun. Here, even if I "accidentally" find myself on the other side of the Glenarm River from the forest, on the grounds of Glenarm Castle, the worst I fear is a reprimand from the current Lady Dunluce.

Do all city people who move to the country feel incongruous, inappropriate, out of place? Do we all worry that we are a disrup-tion to an otherwise harmonious ecosystem, whose homegrown humans do not impose upon its other lives, its hills and meadows, bees and beetles, plumes of purple foxglove and blazes of yellow gorse, its hedgehogs, limpets, wagtails, and wrens, its otters and foxes and buzzards and hares?

There have been moments when I've stood in my backyard to watch the cows parade on the hillside in the early evening—the stocky Shorthorns who handle the steep inclines as capably as goats, the big impressive Anguses, and I've thought: *I am from*

New York. And here I am, standing in my backyard, looking at cows.
And then I've thought about Lisa Douglas, the glamorous European socialite played by Eva Gabor in the 1960s sitcom *Green Acres*, forced to relocate from Manhattan to a small, rural American town regrettably called Hooterville, so that her husband, Oliver, whom she loves, can realize his dream of being a farmer. The mere sight of Lisa—swaddled in furs, dripping in jewels, fully made up and bouffanted—is one of the show's recurring gags. She is the answer to the question "What's wrong with this picture?" She is a person out of place—an obvious outsider, both in her appearance and in her speech.

Eddie Albert was wonderful as Oliver, but Gabor is the best thing about *Green Acres*. She's the reason I watched it, the reason anyone watched it. Viewers loved Lisa Douglas, and even the citizens of Hooterville came to love her, too (I doubt we'd have Moira Rose if we hadn't had Lisa Douglas first). But I'm no Lisa Douglas. That kind of glamour, her kind of glamour, overblown as it was, a caricature, a joke, was a kind of glamour I recognized, a kind I could never touch—my mother's kind of glamour.

Since I was a teenager, I have gravitated instead toward what I might call anti-glamour. I respected the boomer-generation back-to-the-landers I met when I lived in California and Vermont, and ones I read about in books and saw in films. I admired idealistic hippies from working-class Brooklyn families, who moved to Maine in the 1960s to study Buddhism and never left, who brought their children up to know how to light campfires with little more than a fistful of sticks and a flash of the eyes and steady gusts of breath; how to plant seeds and tend to their growth according to the phases of the moon; how to bake with buckwheat and yogurt and occasional help from *The Tassajara Bread Book*; how to look after themselves and others; how to be capable; how to be at home in the natural world. I went to a foraging workshop in Vermont, led by a woman who told me she had turned her back on her rich Boston family, dropped out of college, and hitchhiked north. When the third or fourth driver who picked her up deposited her next to a field, she stayed in that field, as though she had been planted there. She built a house on it, and grew a large garden, and in the woods that abutted her field she led herbal medicine and mushroom-gathering walks. An herbalist and healer, a medicine woman, with a soft, thick tangle of brown and gray hair loosely pinned up, tucked under a folded bandanna: how wonderful she was. Her long face was beautiful, with high cheekbones and square jaw and not a spot of makeup.

Those were, still are, the people I wanted and want to be like. That I am of the city is incontrovertible, and I am not ashamed: I no longer want to live in New York, but I will always love New York. This has meant that I sometimes feel unnatural when I am in nature, but that has never stopped me from yearning for it, and seeking it out, because it is also true that I am, as Wordsworth wrote in "Lines Composed a Few Miles Above Tintern Abbey, On Revisiting the Banks of the Wye during a Tour. July 13, 1798"—my desert-island poem if I really had to pick one—"A lover of the meadows and the woods/And mountains." And I always have been, even when I knew them only from stories and poems, and my own imaginings, including my worst nightmares.

. . . .

Until I moved to Glenarm in 2019, my New York life had been interrupted only by a few years in suburban Connecticut, a few seasons in California's Santa Cruz Mountains, and those four years of college in rural Vermont. The only woods I'd known before were a nature preserve forbiddingly called Devil's Den, not far from where my family lived for a time in Connecticut, a favorite spot for spending a day on LSD while playing hooky from school, and a few hiking trails in the Catskill Mountains of upstate New York and the Berkshire Mountains of western Massachusetts, where I went to summer camp for a few seasons. The house I lived in when I was eighteen, in Ben Lomond, California, outside of Santa Cruz, was a one-hundred-year-old log cabin elevated by high stilts, right on top of a fault line. By the time my roommates and I—all fresh off a few seasons of Grateful Dead tours—moved in, it had survived many earthquakes, including the then-recent and extremely destructive 1989 Loma Prieta quake, which killed 63 people and injured at least 3,700 more, and incurred nearly six billion dollars in damage throughout California's central coast.

How had a century-old wooden house on stilts survived such an event? My unscientific answer was that it was protected by the spirit of the woods that surrounded it—the ancient, ferny, wet, and sunlight-dappled woods of fairy tales for which I had longed, safeguarded by its trees, those heroic madrone and sequoia giants. My time in California was mostly unhappy, fraught with uncertainty and depression, but my memories of that forest, and the solace I found there, are good ones, and I am grateful for my time in it.

In Vermont, I walked in the woods almost every day, occasionally even took naps in them, much to my very urban mother's consternation. Never mind Little Red: she had heard stories of abductions, rapes, even murders of *real* young women who dared to walk through woods alone. But in those New England woods, or most of them anyway, I felt safe. There was one patch that felt different from the rest, as though it had a sad story to tell, a wound that wouldn't heal, and whenever I approached it, I asked for its permission. It always granted it, sometimes hesitating for a moment, sometimes not, and I always knew by the dropping of a leaf, the rustling of a squirrel.

Covering less than a thousand acres, Glenarm Forest is not a vast wilderness, a blip compared, for instance, to the eight hundred thousand acres of New England's White Mountain National Forest. But it is more than backyard enough for me, and, like larger forests, like all good forests, it has an enveloping density, a great green richness about it, and that life-giving smell of woodland air, dewy and ferny and clean as fresh dirt. There are two main trails, a high one that climbs uphill until it has led you nowhere in particular, and a low one that lopes along one side of the Glenarm River. I prefer the low road, because of the river, because rivers are life. Across it are the neatly tended grounds of Glenarm Castle, full of fruit trees and meadows and sheep and roving cows. There is a point at which the two paths connect, by way of a short trail and a stairway of sorts dug out of the hillside and flanked by one of the forest's small waterfalls.

These woods feel good to me. I'm sure they have stories to tell, too, and that some of those stories are sad; this is Ireland, and these are its woods. But what I mostly feel in Glenarm Forest is softness, and sweetness, and gentleness. It does not intimidate or overwhelm.

When Mark and I go walking there together, he still laughs when I hear something and go very quiet and make a sudden stop, although he has seen it happen many times. My years of walking in American woods made me vigilant about certain dangers that lurk within them, but which do not exist here. I still haven't let go of that vigilance, and I don't think I ever will.

"No snakes," he says, and pats my back.

"No bears," I say back.

Call and response.

I make a chant. *No snakes! No bears! No snakes! No bears!*

And we keep walking.

Slemish Mountain, the first Irish home of Saint Patrick, who is said to have driven the snakes off this island, is only ten miles from here, toward Ballymena. He was a child, a slave, a shepherd there, alone and isolated.

That this island has few natural predators—that most of them were hunted out of existence long ago—is an environmental tragedy. But it makes for peaceful, untroubled walks. I relax here in a way I never could in Ben Lomond, or the Green Mountains, or on the New York State long trail. There are foxes—I know they're here, but have yet to see one in Glenarm—and martens. In the warm, sunny pandemic spring of 2020, I heard a lot of worried chatter about giant hogweed, an invasive species that resembles harmless plants, like regular hogweed and cow parsley and Queen Anne's lace, but produces painful blisters if its sap gets on your skin and is exposed to sunlight. In all the time I'd spent in Ireland, I had never heard about the perils of giant hogweed before. I sensed that the heightened alarm was generated, in some complex, emotional way, by our collective anxiety about corona-virus, by the dangers that might befall us from even the simplest and best pleasures, like hugging a friend, or touching a plant.

And I've heard stories about caches of paramilitary weaponry buried long ago, about stockpiles of guns, about how some sweet day you might be ambling across a blanket of bluebells one min-ute, and the next . . . boom. Unlikely. But maybe not impossible. Now and then I come upon a few teenagers in the forest and of course I know they're up to no good, because they stop talking and slow down and their posture shifts, and when I say hello they very sheepishly say hello back. Because I was once a teenager up to no good in the woods.

Mid-May, exactly two months into the lockdown. After a few fret-ful weeks of mostly staying in, of too tentative, too short walks along the shore, where Mark has been collecting bits of driftwood and stone to make into sculptures and birdhouses and bug hotels, he and I agree that it is time to go out for a real walk.

Midafternoon, around three o'clock, we step through the high stone gates and cross the threshold that both cleaves the village away from the wilderness, the cultivated from the wild, and cleaves them together. Through that gate, over the threshold, and my foot-fall changes, goes heavier, as if I am more rooted, more bound to this earth.

To our left Mark points out fresh clusters of bluebells. I notice

a tree with small bright yellow blooms, shaped and bunched together like tiny bananas, and make a note to find out, later, what it
is. The perfume of wild garlic is heady, pervasive, almost soporific.
But until we step just a little farther in, and see it, we have no idea:
between us and the low path that lies by the riverbank, the forest
floor is almost a complete, white, pillowy carpet of flowering wild
garlic. Dots upon dots upon dots of white like Swiss lace, layered
upon ferns and nettles, punctuated once in a while by more bluebells, or buttery yellow primrose. It is a scene so beautiful—like
the Grand Canyon, like Paris—that my first reaction is to laugh.
Why not? One of beauty's graces is that it gives joy.

Mark knows the natural world better than I do, and has great
reserves of patience for it. I march farther along the riverside path,
deciding whether or not I should throw myself on a great cushion
of flowering garlic and just stay still there for a spell, the way I
once napped in the Vermont woods. I only notice then that Mark
is not beside me, but still downriver, watching. I turn back and
walk to him.

"Look," he says quietly, and points at a jumping fish. I think of
Yeats's Aengus, wandering the hazel wood, hooking a berry to a
thread, dropping it in the stream, catching a silver trout.

We continue to walk together. A funny little yellow wagtail—
how can it not be funny?—wiggles and wags and bops on a large
slick stone. He's showing off. It's a mating dance.

We continue, and we are quiet. Occasionally we bend to cut
some wild garlic with Mark's pocketknife, for our dinner. At home,
people called it "ramps" and paid a fortune for it at the farmers'
market and I thought it was ridiculous. Until now, I'd never eaten
the flowers, never even known that they were edible. They are

delicious. This whole thing, this walk, these woods, the human and nonhuman company, it is all delicious. Yeats comes to mind again: the piercing of the deep wood's woven shade, the having of some peace, the child stolen by fairies and taken by hand to the waters and the wild. And later, when I share pictures of the day's walk with friends back home, many of them do not hesitate to ask: *Are there fairies there?* Some are joking, some are not.

"Of course there are," I tell them.

Later, I'll tell them the truth: there may be fairies in Glenarm Forest, but anyone here will tell you that the real spot for fairies is another Glenarm woodland, Straidkilly. And they'll tell you the story about the village woman who was summoned to Straidkilly to assist in a fairy birth. It was Mona Hyndman who first told me the story. "I'm not sure I got it right," she said, and urged me to look up other versions, such as those written down by Felix McKillop and Jack McBride, who claims that the story is "the first folk-tale about a human midwife for a fairy birth"—though many versions exist around the world.

This is what happened. A Glenarm girl was widely esteemed as a midwife. Late one night, she awakened to knocking on her door. Looking down, she saw a fairy in a state of agitation. "You must come with me," he told her, and ushered her into a carriage. When the horses stopped, the driver dismounted and blindfolded the midwife. He led her to a cave and removed her mask. She saw a magnificent, tiny castle before her, and was led to a room inside it. There lay a lady fairy no more than three feet high, suffering in her labor. Hours later, the Glenarm midwife safely delivered a healthy baby boy—"The smallest wee morsel she had ever seen."

She thought she'd be taken home now, but was told she must

stay a few weeks longer, until the fairy queen was back on her feet again. She was assured that her chickens, her cow, and her goat would be looked after.

"I'll stay," she said, as if she had a choice. "On one condition. You must bring me food from the human world. I will not eat faery food." She knew, as all humans knew, that anyone who eats fairy food can be imprisoned by the fairies forever. The fairies agreed, and brought her only the finest human food.

Only days before she was to return to the village, the midwife was given a special oil to anoint the baby. Afterward, she rubbed her right eye, and got some of the oil in it. In an instant, she was back in her cottage. There was a giant purse full of gold coins on her bed. And instead of one cow, she now had two. And two goats, not just one. The fairies had paid her handsomely for her services.

Later that day, in the village shop, she saw two fairies loading their baskets and making to leave without paying. When she accused them of stealing, one dropped his basket. "You can see us?" he asked.

"I can, so."

"With both eyes?"

She closed one and then the other.

"Only the right."

"That's lucky for you," said the fairy man, and punched her hard in the right eye, which stayed blind forever after. And when the midwife got home, there was only one goat. One horse. And no gold coins.

That's the way it is with Irish fairies. There's nothing cute about them—they are cunning, and tough, and protect only their own interests. But to do this to a healer? To the woman who saved the fairy queen and her child? Here, in Glenarm? I take the story personally, and it angers me. I have come here for healing, and without gold or goats or horses to offer, I can only give thanks.

After our walk in the garlic-carpeted woods, Mark and I come home, make tea, stand together at the kitchen window, and watch Stan weave in and out of the excellent birdhouse Mark has made of driftwood and twine. Two coal tits flit, then alight briefly on the laundry line. A jackdaw shows up—it annoys Mark that he drives the smaller birds away, but I think he is intelligent and beautiful, in his velvety plumage, a chiaroscuro of black and grays.

Why are you doing this? *Why are you leaving* here? *Why are you going* there?

I can still hear the questions my friends and relatives asked me before I left New York. They tangle with my own. *Do I belong here? Where is my home? Is this it?*

I answer these questions when I go through the gates and enter the forest. I answer them when I walk along the shoreline. I answer that *this* is why. The forest is why I am here. The sea is why I am here. This is why.

I hear the questions sometimes when I wake up Mark, who will sleep at least four hours longer than I could ever bear to, allowing me my quiet and sacred and solitary morning time. Before I go downstairs to make my coffee and start my day, I watch him turn toward the side of the bed I have only just left, and reach out as if I might still be there. This is also why I am here. This nature, too.

"The witchery of Irish waterfalls is well known," writes Jack McBride, in *Traveller in the Glens*, his 1979 narrative tour of the region. "They have not the awe-inspiring grandeur of a Niagara or Zambesi fall, but for enchanting loveliness they are unequalled."

Glenarm Forest has its own modestly enchanting waterfalls, but this morning in June I have awakened early to take a bus to Carnlough Harbour with my friend Jacky. From there, we will walk just about a mile and a half to Cranny Falls—a place I've been meaning to get to for almost a year, but to which I hadn't yet made it. About a month earlier, I'd gone alone, and after more than a mile, when I could only have been another few minutes away, I turned back. I reasoned that not knowing the terrain— was it steep? was it slippery? was it safe?—I shouldn't go alone. What if my poor arthritic knees gave out and I fell, with no one around? What if I hurt myself, and then wasted the National Health Service's precious resources during a pandemic? I wouldn't be that person. I would be responsible and go home—and return to Cranny Falls another day, and not on my own.

That's how I reasoned with myself. But I don't think it's really why I got so close and then turned back.

In the eighteenth century, Cranny Falls, now part of the village of Carnlough, would have been part of one great, wild swath of woodland hugging the Antrim Coast. And this is why some say that the last native Irish wolf was killed in Glenarm, not Carnlough, in 1712. It happened at Cranny Falls. No other details have survived the centuries (and it is not the only "last wolf" story in Ireland: others are set on the border of Kilkenny and Tipperary, in County Carlow, even in Belfast). We will never know for sure where the last Irish wolf lived and died—but Cranny Falls is as good a contender as any. I knew this, and it's the knowing this that kept me from visiting the falls by myself.

Why should I be worried about a place where a wolf might have died three hundred years ago? It makes no sense. By now, it is good and dead, long gone. But I wonder if its spirit still lingers there. If it does, wouldn't it be a profoundly sad spirit? Hated, hunted, extinguished.

Jacky comes with me, and we set out early in the morning. We walk little more than ten minutes out of Carnlough—a bustling village with a busy harbor, a post office, a few cafés and Chinese food takeaways and a pharmacy and even a library—and we are in deep country. A few old farmhouses are scattered on hillsides high above the sea. Sheep graze the meadows. Hawthorn trees— they are sacred to fairies and must never be cut down or otherwise messed with—are profusely in flower, some white, some pink. I've seen about a dozen blackbirds on this not-long walk, a few robins, some butterflies. An unfamiliar purple flower that looks tropical. Some tangled bushes of thorny wild roses.

We walk deeper into what had been wolf territory, and are disappointed that we won't be able to see the waterfall: the trail ends now at two stern gates, one behind the other, put up after landslides a few years ago. But we have heard the music of the falls, and the streams they feed, all along the trail. We don't linger long—we both have busy days ahead of us.

Like Glenarm Forest, Cranny Falls feels both wild and gentle to me at once—much like the version of "The Last Wolf" story written and told by my friend Colin Urwin. In Colin's telling, the last wolf is actually a man cursed to live as a wolf. He ambushes a priest traveling alone through the Glens, so that his dying wife, a she-werewolf, may receive last rites. The wolf does no harm to the priest and directs him, as promised, to the safety of the village of Carnlough. There, the priest betrays him: he tells the men of the village that he was attacked by a wolf, now sleeping beside Cranny Falls. For the thrill and the bounty, the men head to the falls with their muskets. It is a sad story, and is, at its heart, a love story.

Back on the path toward Carnlough, an old man walks his two dogs some distance ahead of us. One of his dogs, a German pointer, does his job: he hears Jacky and me, turns around, looks us over, turns again, and alerts his master to our presence. The old man waves and we wave back. The pointer and the other dog, a springer spaniel, decide we're okay, and bound toward us. We reward them with pets and rubs and praise, then walk beside them and the old man for a while. He has the accent and speech of a Glens farmer; he is friendly and happy for the company—especially the company of fellow dog lovers.

We could talk and walk together for hours, but Jacky and I have to catch the next bus to Glenarm from Carnlough Harbour; there won't be another for hours. We must head back to our village. We must go home.

11

WHEN FRANK DIED AND MY MOTHER WAS TOO unwell to come to the funeral, I asked her to promise me that she wouldn't die that year, too. She made me that promise and she kept it. She died one year and thirteen days after Frank.

I hadn't read the Irish writer Anne Enright until her novel *The Green Road* was assigned reading in my MA program at Queen's. I started the book on the bus back to Glenarm from Belfast one evening, and walked back to my house still gripping it in my hand, unable to let go. I devoured the rest of it that night, after I'd thrown some dinner together, lighted a fire in the hearth, and settled into the warm quiet of my living room.

If my main reason for returning to school at age forty-eight was purely practical—it was the most straightforward path to a visa that would make a long and uninterrupted stay in Glenarm possible—I was excited about it anyway. I knew I stood to learn much from being in a classroom again, from having a physical and psychic space carved out only for writing and reading, and for thinking and talking about both. All that proved true—and being back in school gave me another gift, one I hadn't expected:

assigned reading. I really enjoyed being told what to read, after so many years on the assigning side of the classroom.

The Green Road's main character, Rosaleen Madigan, is a difficult woman, a difficult mother. She is described as "impossible," and "maddening." She is easily wounded. She is needy, and bossy. She is vain, and she can be petty, and she can be cruel, especially to those closest to her, those upon whom she relies and who rely upon her, her four children.

Rosaleen's indignations and unkindnesses multiply and thicken until finally she is cast out, alone, on the green road that gives the book its title, in a poignant and harrowing scene of disorientation and human fragility reminiscent of King Lear on the storm-racked heath; earlier in the novel, she echoes Lear, when she signs off on a Christmas card to one of her sons, "Your fond and foolish Mother, Rosaleen."

I first saw *King Lear* when I was a teenager, in Peter Brook's version for the BBC (Paul Scofield remains *my* Lear, the great Lear, with his cartographic face and dark, dimming eyes, his long silences), and I predictably saw my father in Lear; it is sometimes said that *King Lear* is a play for daughters, *Hamlet* for sons. My father had twice the number of children Lear had, and not all girls—four daughters and two sons—with three wives. He had, one could say, with each marriage and with each divorce, divided a small kind of kingdom. Once, when I called him from college to ask for some advice on finishing my senior thesis—he had written at least twenty books by then—he said, "I wish I could help you, kid, but alimony is my muse."

Like Lear, my father expected actions by which his children showed their love for him, and words that expressed it, too. Feeling injured, and misunderstood, I related to Cordelia: I loved my father, according to our bond, and I would not heave my heart into my mouth to say so—not until very late, when he was, suddenly and unexpectedly, dying, at the age of sixty-eight, at the end of 2001, in the long season of 9/11, the result of complications from hip-replacement surgery.

At my father's funeral, without bitterness, I quoted *King Lear* in my eulogy for him. But in the years that followed, when I took in every possible production of the play staged in New York City, I didn't stop seeing my father in the king, but I started to see my mother, whom I knew much better, to whom I was much closer, and who surpassed my father in both fondness and foolishness. And I saw her, too, in Rosaleen Madigan—with whom she is united, like King Lear, by the very particular tragedy of having grown old without having grown wise.

My mother, who owned almost nothing at the time of her death, who had piled up debt for most of her adult life, had made no will—but had many times expressed her desire that only my brother and I attend her funeral. She had alienated, or otherwise grown estranged from, many friends and most other relatives by the time she died. I can't remember what I said at her small funeral. Did I say anything? Would I have read a eulogy only for my brother to hear? What would I have said?

I had spent her last day, and the night of the death, with her at a hospital in the Bronx—still guilty that I had not been at Frank's bedside when the moment of death came for him, just one year earlier, and I would not allow myself to be absent when that moment arrived for my mother. I could not bear the thought of her dying alone, too. And, for all the anguish and difficulty that had defined our relationship, I also could not bear the thought of her leaving the world without hearing the words "I love you" again. I said them to her, over and over, that last night, as I held her hand, her skin thin and dry as papyrus.

I remembered a story she had often told me about my birth, when, moments after I had emerged from her body, the obstetrician lifted me up and said, "She has beautiful hands."

"That's nice," Ma said. "But how's the face?"

More than midway through *The Green Road*, Enright writes: "'It's a very hard thing,' said Rosaleen finally. 'To describe your mother.'" Here, the author, who writes mothers so well, slyly concedes the difficulty of the undertaking. And it is only now, more than a decade after the death of my mother, far from home, in a country she never visited, that I am perhaps as ready as I ever will be to try.

In the summer of 2018 when I was still living in New York, a woman, an old family friend whom I had not seen or spoken with since I was five years old, sent me a message:

> *I'm in NY 'til 7/25 and would love to buy you lunch to catch up after so many years. I spent so much time with you, your mom, and Jeremy from the time you were born 'til we moved to LA in 1976.*

I remembered her warmly, and her late husband, and their two daughters, not far in age from my brother and me. I wrote back immediately and we made a date.

194

We met for brunch at a café in Greenwich Village. She brought with her a copy of my first book and asked me to sign it—a nice thing to do. "Your mother would be so proud of you," she said—a nice thing to say, and she meant it. In 2008, when I started writing that book, my mother was alive. When it came out in 2013, she was not. I don't know if she would have been proud of me, of it.

"When are you gonna write about *me*?" she often asked.

"What do you think, Ma?" I always called her "ma," which sounds so old-fashioned, so unapologetically "ethnic." WASPs don't call their mothers "ma." Jews do. (And so do Irish people).

"When I'm dead."

"When you're dead."

And we'd have a good laugh.

I didn't have to fill in the old family friend. She'd read my first book; she knew what I'd been up to. She knew I'd married a man who died too young. She knew that for a long time I drank a lot, but that those days were over. She knew I'd gotten a steady job and lived in Brooklyn. She knew that my politics were much like her own, and that she wouldn't find herself sitting across a table from a fuming forty-seven-year-old woman in a MAGA hat.

But she didn't know how hard things had gotten for my mother, how sick she was and for so long, or how fraught our relationship had been.

"No one was more fun than Madeleine," she said. "No one was like her. I miss her."

Everything she said was true, or had once been true. But it was also true that since my mother had died in 2011, although I thought about her often, I didn't miss her. My life was lighter without her, as though, perhaps, its heaviest weight had lifted. These are terrible things to say, and there was no reason for me to say them to her old friend, who thought so well, and only well, of her. Why would I not let her remember my mother as she did, which was the way she would have wished to be remembered: funny, beautiful, singular, vivacious—suspended in the amber of 1976, only two years before my father left and her fragile heart cracked apart and was never mended, before what was bad got worse, much worse?

Not long after our brunch, the woman sent me an envelope full of pictures of my mother, all new to me. In this windfall of extraordinary images, one stood out. It could be a still from a French New Wave film: my mother in 1966, wearing a boxy, boat-necked sweater and enormous black sunglasses—casually chic, very Courrèges. She's leaning against a thickly stuccoed wall somewhere in California. Her full lips are pulled into a pout, and glossed a very mod white-pink. She was probably about to say something, or was in mid-sentence; she was a talker. With one hand she clutches a thick hank of her blunt black bob. Her skin is creamy and smooth, freckled across her strong nose.

She was a great beauty.

That's a thing people say about some women. But she was.

I tucked the photograph between two pieces of cardboard and slipped it into a manila folder. I took it with me to Ireland, in my carry-on bag. When I arrived in Glenarm, I framed it, and my mother looks at me through those enormous black sunglasses from a side table in my living room, close to the hearth. She always loved an open fire. I brought another photo of her, too—a small one, from the winter of 1968. She's standing outside the

Grosvenor House hotel in London, on her first, and only, trip there. The same pale lipstick. A gray fur collar of some kind. Dark brows, boldly lined eyes. I keep it on a shelf in the dining room now. She used to display it on a side table in her living room. "Why do you have a picture of Elizabeth Taylor in your house?" visitors sometimes asked her. She loved that, too.

When my mother was young, her own mother told her that it was a good thing that she was beautiful because she wasn't very bright and extinguished any hope my mother had of going to college, so my mother went to drama school instead. But she always read; she loved books. She liked to write, too. I think she would have loved college. I'm sorry she didn't go.

She could be defensive about her intelligence and would rail against her children: "You two think you're so much smarter than me." We didn't. But having been raised by a mother who told her she was dumb, how could she not have doubts?

"If I'd been taught everything in songs," she often said, "I'd know everything. People would think I'm a genius." Yes, she was a song savant. She knew thousands of lyrics by heart.

After drama school, she got small roles on stage, bit parts in movies, walk-ons on television programs, a stint as a game-show hostess. She had flings with famous men—one of whom gave her a drawing by Velázquez, which she pawned for little, not aware of its worth. Another gave her an emerald-and-diamond swizzle stick from Van Cleef & Arpels; she pawned that, too.

She wanted to be a star. She also wanted to be a mother, and that one might be a movie star and a mother at once was not a calculation most women of her generation dared to make.

When she spoke of her own mother, she always said, *"Mother" is only half a word*, leaving me to guess the other half.

From my bedroom off the hallway in the back of our apartment, I heard them fighting. Through tears and short quick breaths I heard my mother say to my father:

"I hope your balls fall off."

It was 1978; I was seven. None of this was new. The only days that passed without a fight were when my father was away on business trips, or pretending he was. I was used to the fights. But now I heard my father begging: *No, no, no.* That was new.

I ran to the living room. My mother gripped a glass paperweight in the shape of a porcupine, heavy as a sack of sugar, sharp and pointy as an awl. She aimed it at his head and I thought she might kill him.

He was still on his knees, abject. *No. No. No.*

I ran back down the hall and unlocked the back door. "This way," I called to my father, and I held the door open wide. He went through it and flew down six flights of stairs and never came back. And Ma never let me forget it.

In the early 2000s, I worked for a homeless services agency in Manhattan. My cubicle was close to a caseworker's. I often overheard her meeting with her clients, many of whom were single mothers living with their children in cold, crowded city shelters. One woman had a criminally violent boyfriend, who was in and out of prison. She knew he was trouble, but she couldn't cut him loose.

Her caseworker warned that he was not only a danger to her, but also a danger to her two small daughters. And because he was dangerous, and because she persisted in letting him into their lives, child protective services might come and take the girls away.

"They can't take my babies."

Oh yes, they can, her caseworker said.

"I'm a good mother," the woman said, adding to support this: "I love my babies."

She sounded like my mother, to whom motherhood meant: *I love my children.* Who loved her children, and who wanted to believe that love supplanted recklessness and rage, instability and fear. Who needed the solace of thinking that love alone is enough.

I had to read Euripides's *Medea* in high school. In this furious ancient woman, who kills her own children to take revenge on their father, her unfaithful husband, I saw my mother.

"I have a new nickname for you," I told her after I'd finished reading the play.

She'd read it in drama school, but had not been cast as Medea. The role she always talked about from her student days was Masha, in Chekhov's *The Seagull.* My mother often recited to me Masha's most famous lines: *I am in mourning for my life. I am unhappy.*

I thought that calling her Medea might lead her to reflection. I also thought it would hurt her. Instead, she burst into laughter. Nothing mattered more to her than being funny, as long as you weren't funnier than she was, and no one ever was.

"That's a good line," she said.

A sniffle, a touch of fever, a slight scratchy cough: any of these would do if I didn't want to go to school, and I never wanted to go to school. My mother would call the secretary and tell her I was very sick, too sick to get out of bed. Then we'd get dressed, get in a taxi, and go to Eighth Avenue.

At the pawnshop, a gold ring might get a hundred bucks. A good watch, even more. After, we'd go around the corner to Patsy's on Fifty-Sixth Street, whose black-and-white checkerboard floors were immaculate and shinier than mirrors, whose big white linen napkins were spotless and stiff as corpses. I had the cheese ravioli, she had the veal rollatini. The waiters and owners knew her name. Sal hugged her; Joey kissed her hand. When she was little, Mama Patsy, the matriarch, let my mother's family eat in the kitchen while she cooked, and fed my mother sauce straight from the burbling pot with a wooden spoon, and cooed at the beautiful curly-headed toddler who already had the sense and good taste to appreciate her cooking.

After lunch we'd turn onto Broadway, and walk one block north to the Coliseum Bookshop, where she let me pick out two books, sometimes more, and she'd get one for herself.

When she wanted company and let me play hooky and we went

to the pawnshop and had a little cash, we never fought. And on days like those, I loved her so much.

My mother expected the neighbors to greet us with homemade pies, casseroles, and open arms when we moved to the suburbs. They did not. A divorced woman with a theatrical disposition, enormous breasts, and a foul mouth was not someone whose company they welcomed. Many mornings, she woke up early, made us breakfast, then returned to her bed. She stayed there all day, watching talk shows and eating bagsful of Hershey's Kisses and smoking Parliaments and sipping coffee that had gone cold from a ceramic beer stein. *I am unhappy. I am in mourning for my life.*

That she was uncommonly sexual, and uncommonly open about sex, was obvious, and it made many people uncomfortable, especially her daughter. I knew about her good lovers, and the bad ones. And she could have put more clothes on more often. I didn't need my friends to see all that when she reached into the fridge to find the Dijon mustard. She said she just didn't like underwear.

But the same friends who might have been unnerved by the sight of my half-naked mother, by all the racket and mayhem of our home, by the six cats and two dogs and mad-eyed parrot she had taken in, they adored her, almost to a person.

If you were kicked out, Madeleine took you in, like another stray. If you were hungry, she fed you, and fed you well.

201

When I told her that a friend's parents had forgotten their daughter's birthday, my mother said, "Call her and tell her to be here at six." She called a bakery and ordered a cake with buttercream roses and "Happy Birthday" piped on top, and started cooking, and made a party for my latchkey-kid friend. I always wished I was a latchkey kid. Or in boarding school.

Another friend had run away from her father, who had hit her, hard and often. I was sixteen and she was fifteen when we went to a Grateful Dead show together in New Jersey, then lingered late in the parking lot after, drinking beer and getting high and singing songs with long-haired boys strumming guitars. We'd agreed before the show that she would spend the night at my house. She hadn't met my ma.

It was very late, after three, when I pushed my key quietly into the front door. When it swung open, Ma was standing on the other side. Her face, beautiful in repose, could be frightening in anger: a heat map of overstimulated capillaries and veins, reddened by rage. A sharp smack across my jaw came first. Then a powerful push to the floor.

My friend ran quickly into the next room to hide.

I hadn't called. She thought I was dead.

Another smack, and again. A tight pull on my long, tangled hair.

"If you were worried I was dead, why are you trying to kill me?"

Her fury finally exhausted her, and she went to bed.

My friend curled herself small in a sleeping bag in the corner of my bedroom. I moved my desk in front of the door.

It was okay, I told my friend in the morning, it was fine, and coaxed her into the kitchen. My mother made soft buttery scrambled eggs and buttered rye toast. We three sat together at the breakfast table. We ate and talked about boys and Ma told her favorite dirty jokes, which were very dirty. *Marty and Helen went on a hike in Palm Springs. Well, they sat down on a rock, and suddenly a rattlesnake leapt up and bit Marty on his cock . . .* is how one started.

We drank coffee and smoked cigarettes and laughed. My friend hugged her tightly before she left.

In college I spent as much time as I could in the woods. In autumn I'd stray from the trails to sink one heavy hiking boot and then the next into high piles of leaves; my reward was the grounding pleasure of a deep crunch underfoot. When the sky started to darken around me, tilting from lilac toward indigo, then I'd head back to my dorm.

Jenny, my roommate, would tell me about any calls I missed (this was long before everyone had cell phones) on our shared phone. They were mostly from my mother. And Jenny, a blunt New Englander who always said it like she saw it, had told me more than once that my mother was not happy that I was spending so much time in the woods.

Jenny's impersonation of my mother was funny, but not charitable. It was a chain-smoker's screech. It was a squawk. It was gurgly and guttural and suggested to me the noise a cartoon pterodactyl might make when swooping in on lizard prey. A cartoon pterodactyl, with the diction and rough manners of a Brooklyn cabbie circa 1957.

Jenny took wicked pleasure in recounting her telephone conversations with my mother. In her dramatic reenactments, she
artfully exaggerated her own politesse to underscore my mother's
stunning rude harshness.

"Hello, this is Jennifer. To whom am I speaking?"

"You know who this is."

"Oh hello, Madeleine. How are—"

"Where is she?"

"I believe she said she was going to the woods, Madeleine."

"She's from *New York*. What is she doing in *the woods*?"

"I believe she said something about communing with trees,
Madeleine."

"She could get *killed*. Or *raped*."

"I'm sure she's—"

"If she gets back alive, have her call me."

"I'll be sure to pass along your message, Madeleine."

Click.

But when I returned from a forest ramble one evening, Jenny
looked stricken, not eager to recap that evening's chat with Madeleine.

"Is she okay?"

"She is *not* okay."

I could tell from her tone that my mother hadn't died.

My first thought was that she'd been arrested.

But slowly, what it was that Jenny meant started to sink in. She
was trying to tell me: *Your mother is not sane.* I inferred that she
was also trying to tell me that it wasn't healthy for me to persist in
pretending that she was.

My mother had kept Jenny on the phone that night for hours,

and had delivered a disjointed, unbroken monologue. Jenny did not use the word "manic," but years later, when my mother received for the first time a diagnosis of bipolar disorder, I sensed that that's what she had been then. And that those long sad days in Connecticut, when she sometimes left her bed only for breakfast and dinner, those were times when she'd swung to the other end.

She was volatile, vain, and reckless. But when people who didn't know her asked about her, I didn't want to go into all that—why would I?—and just said she was eccentric. I must have known that she was sick. But I couldn't—

When I finally could, after that conversation with Jenny, I started to soften. We still fought. I kept distance between us. There were months when we didn't speak at all. But I had accepted the possibility that she had done her best, and that she really believed that loving her children was the soul of motherhood, the only thing that mattered.

Her dying was long and miserable.

A few years before the end, she had a full psychotic break, resulting not only from the disease that had been troubling her mind for so long, but compounded by medications—for heart disease, high blood pressure, diabetes, depression, and nerve damage—which she often, not intentionally, mixed up, and with which she sometimes under- or overmedicated herself. (There had been so much medication, so many bottles, so many pillboxes: she'd nod toward her bedside table and say, "*The Valley of the Dolls.*")

When our calls went unanswered and we hadn't heard from her

in days, my brother drove us to her house, where we found a stack of newspapers on her doorstep, and, inside, a hungry and smelly and bewildered cat. The sight of the cat stiffened me with fear: even when she could hardly take care of us, or herself, my mother never neglected her pets, never left them alone, unfed, sick, afraid.

We found our mother in a psychiatric hospital a few towns away, and learned that she had been discovered one night wandering the streets of her town, barely clothed, speaking in what sounded like riddles, and had asked a stranger she encountered: *Are you a rabbi?*

After the psychotic break, she moved into an assisted living place closer to the city.

Frank and I took the cat.

I spent a lot of time with her during those last few years. There was no need to fight anymore. We held hands and sang, and I read to her.

A Sunday morning in Glenarm, and I'm in the kitchen listening to Johnny Cash sing about another Sunday morning, somewhere else. It's almost summer, the time of year when I start to have pangs of longing for certain things, American things: sunny-day cookouts, Brighton Beach picnics, lemonade and fried chicken. Really good fried chicken, which I have not found in Northern Ireland.

My mother made the most delicious fried chicken—maybe surprising for a native New Yorker, but I'd put it up against any Kentuckian's fried chicken. It's not exactly a recipe, but here's what I remember from watching her countless times: She didn't brine. She put a very large quantity of flour very generously seasoned with salt, pepper, and paprika in a very large (*clean!*) garbage bag, mysteriously tossed in a trayful of ice cubes, added the chicken pieces, shook them up and down in the flour mixture a few times, then stuffed the trash bag full of seasoned chicken into the fridge and let it sit there for a while. Then she set up her two electric frying pans, which were only ever used for this purpose. One had a broken leg, so she propped it up on a couple of cans of tuna or cat food.

The cooking fat was always mostly Crisco (the kind in tubs) and some bacon grease or a few slices of bacon just tossed into the Crisco as it melted. As soon as the oil came up to temperature, she pulled a stool up to the counter right in front of the pans, sat down, and started slowly, patiently frying, a few pieces a time in each pan. She turned the pieces frequently with a long, two-pronged fork, inspecting each angle for the right color.

A big ceramic bowl thickly lined with paper towels sat nearby, ready for each perfect golden-brown piece she pulled from the hot oil; it was my job to change the paper towels at regular intervals. She never used a timer or a thermometer, judged doneness entirely according to color, and was never wrong.

There was always an ashtray on the counter, because she smoked while she fried chicken—it was a long process, as she usually cooked at least three chickens' worth at a go, allowing plenty for guests and for leftovers and for late-night and early morning refrigerator raids.

She always insisted that the butcher include the livers, so she fried those first and we snacked on them and chatted while she cooked up the rest of the chicken.

I love to cook, but I've always hated any frying job that requires more than an inch of hot oil, so I almost never make fried chicken. It had been years—at least ten—but the day arrived. I couldn't make it exactly like Ma did. I don't have electric frying pans, and my hot-oil phobia meant I used a deep Dutch oven. The high smoking point of peanut oil felt safer to me, and I figured a good soak in buttermilk couldn't hurt.

Most of all, I don't have her particular magic, her touch, her confidence and ease in frying. But I was patient with it, like she was, and it turned out just fine.

Jenny's impersonations of my mother were as painful to me as they were funny because Jenny didn't know that my mother could also be good, could also be soft. I hadn't told her that my mother's voice didn't always sound like that, that it could also be beautiful. That she often sang to my brother and me when we were children, with style, and restraint, and sensitivity.

At bath time when we were still small enough to share a bath, we wanted to hear songs from the musical *Oklahoma!*, and she belted them out with good cheer and a fake, cowpoke accent: "Everything's up to date in Kansas City."

When I was older, and my mother and I did the dishes together most nights after dinner, it was usually some Cole Porter, Jerome

Kern, a little Gershwin, including her favorite, "Love Is Here to Stay," and mine, "Someone to Watch Over Me."

I don't mind singing alone, but her voice made mine sound better.

Is it true that I don't miss her? Do I mean it?

My life is easier without her, without worrying about her, which I did, always, even if she didn't know it: a low vibration in my spine, an anxious hum, an uneasy alertness that something was wrong, was always wrong.

Sometimes when I'm at my kitchen sink in Glenarm, doing the dishes, I wish that she was here, singing with me. And I try to imagine what she would make of this life I've chosen—in a place so small, so far, in so many ways, from New York City. She had never been to Ireland, but she always felt affectionate toward it, always wished she had visited (her only overseas trip, for her honeymoon in 1968, started in England and ended with a terrifying flight home from Spain that made her never want to board a plane again). The Ireland my mother imagined was the place in *The Quiet Man*, the place sung about by the Clancy Brothers in their big fishermen's cable-knit sweaters, the place with the blarney and the leprechauns and the pots of gold at the ends of rainbows, and the affable inebriated men—she'd met a few in New York pubs—with deeply cleft chins and stockpiles of sentimental stories. She loved that Ireland. And as much as I have resisted that version of it, I felt no need to take it from her and replace it with something like the truth.

One August, not long after she'd moved into assisted living, I was in Dublin. On the thirtieth, her birthday, I was sitting outside my favorite pub there, Grogan's, sharing a table with strangers. I called her to wish her "Happy Birthday," and every person at every table around me joined in. She loved being sung to, and celebrated, by a crowd of Irish strangers and me.

"Your mother would be so proud of you," I remember her kind friend saying at that café in Greenwich Village. Would she? Or would she think I've just run away, from someone, from something, again? I had run away from her many times. I had quit school, more than once. I had gotten bored, or frustrated, or scared, and quit. Would she see this move to a village by the sea as a big, bold leap, as the discovery, finally, of what I needed most—or as another escape?

I think she would get it: the humor. The *craic*.

And most of all, the sea. When I walk or sit by the water, I wish that she could see that view. My mother, who had spent the summers of her youth on Fire Island, loved the sea, maybe as much as she loved her own children.

The forest: that, she could do without.

Don't worry, Ma. Rest. I'm happy here.

12

LITTLE HAD CHANGED IN GLENARM WHEN I RE-
turned for my second visit in 2017. The crafts shop down the lane
from the Barbican was still open, still selling locally made willow
baskets and pottery and hand-turned wooden spoons, and, on the
weekend, sourdough bread kneaded, shaped, and baked by the
owner. The small village store was still up and running, even if its
inventory had diminished. Both of the pubs—the Bridge End and
the Coast Road—still seemed busy enough, serving their regulars
and the punters passing through.

But Stevey's pub, the Bridge End, the one I liked so much that
it was among the things that made me like the village enough
to come back, felt different in a small but good way—lighter,
brighter, as though windows that had been glued shut had finally
been opened. There were pots of colorful flowers in the courtyard.
And Stevey himself seemed a little less gruff; even if that gruffness
had mostly been a mask, he had let the mask down.

What had happened? It wasn't only roses and heather that had
blossomed—love had, too. Stevey had a girlfriend.

I first saw Joan in the pub on a busy Saturday night. It was impossible not to notice the smiling, blond woman with "Brook-lyn" written in big letters on her shirt. I wanted to go over to her and tell her that the place whose name was splashed across her tee was my home, but I hesitated, and decided not to; sometimes I'm grateful for an easy conversation starter—*Oh have you been? Do you have family there?*—sometimes I feel awkward, forced, even showy. Besides, maybe she was working and it would be an unwelcome interruption; I couldn't tell. Instead, I watched her table-hopping, grinning, joking—and I liked her instantly; before I even knew who she was, I knew she was warm and energetic. I figured she was probably a year or two younger than me, and although I couldn't place her accent exactly, I suspected that she was also a "blow-in," but from not so far away, from somewhere just over the border in the Republic of Ireland.

I wouldn't call Joan an extrovert, but she's friendly and open, and a great conversationalist—both as talker and as listener. When she asked me what had brought me to Glenarm, I intuited that I could tell her, without shame or hesitation, that by then I believed that loss had something to do with it. I told her about Frank's death, and my mother's, and about my feeling that I'd gotten mourning wrong.

And she told me about her son, Matthew, who died in a car accident, age twenty-one, in 2013.

We are not meant to make a hierarchy of loss, to weigh one suffering against another. We are not meant to consider all losses the same, neither are we meant to consider all losses dramatically and inherently different. Such comparisons feel distasteful, unfair, wrongheaded, and wronghearted. But when Joan said the words "son" and "died," a knot gathered in my chest. I thought about

Frank's parents, and how I felt, when he died, that as bereft as I was, their loss was deeper and more excruciating than my own. I remembered the devastated parents I had met when I was a Red Cross volunteer after 9/11, some of whom I accompanied to Ground Zero and held while they wept: *my baby, my baby*. To out-live your child: it isn't natural, it isn't fair, it isn't the way of things, it's not the proper ordering of events. And, rightly or wrongly, I still feel that way: that this is the loss beyond loss, which no other grief can equal, certainly not my own.

I felt privileged by Joan's disclosure, touched that someone I'd only recently and casually met would hold the door open to such pain, her pain, and trust me enough to let me come through. And I admired, was even awed by, the openness and clarity with which she spoke of Matthew—"*my funny, handsome boy*"—and her love for him, and the depth of her grief in his absence. It was the kind of openness I had myself been reaching for and maybe getting closer to, especially whenever I was in Ireland—in part because I saw it enacted here more often, and more fully, than I had seen back home.

When I moved here in 2019, I was thrilled, but not surprised, to see that Joan and Stevey were still going strong, and that Joan had officially left Letterkenny, the Donegal town where she had lived for more than twenty years, where she had raised Matthew and his big sister, Naoimi, and moved to Glenarm. Even more of her personal touches were evident in the pub: still more flowers were blooming in the courtyard, there was new blue upholstery on the benches inside, fresh lace curtains on the windows. The upstairs lounge was the tidiest I'd ever seen it, and the ladies' loo felt like less of an afterthought.

On many evenings, she and Stevey worked side by side behind the bar, in that relaxed rhythm familiar to anyone who's ever had to share that narrow space behind the taps—steady, harmonious, one taking orders, the other filling pints, one shaking up whipping cream for Irish coffees, the other quietly disappearing out back to change a keg. Stevey may have been master of the Bridge End for more than thirty years, but Joan was now not only part of the life of it, she had improved and enriched its life, and fixed something no one ever thought had been broken.

I was also happy to discover that by then Joan had joined Sue's Tuesday evening yoga class at Seaview Primary School—and loved it. In 2017, I usually saw her in the pub after class, and, like others, suggested she might enjoy it. Back then, she seemed to think that yoga wasn't for her, and I sensed an intimation not only of class consciousness, but of class self-consciousness. Joan felt, she later told me, that yoga was for a certain kind of person, a kind of person she was not. I was glad she'd changed her mind about that.

And I was grateful that, when I told her I was writing about grief, and about Glenarm, Joan was willing to talk to me about her own move to the village, and about her own devastating loss. I knew it could be painful for her to talk about Matthew, but I also knew that she took pleasure in talking about him, and solace from it. To speak his name, to tell his stories, to describe his laughter and his hair and his friends, to imitate his voice: these do not return him from death, but they keep him present among the living. To love is to remember; to remember is to keep loving.

On a blustery October day, Joan came over to my house to chat. The COVID pandemic had long since begun, and we sat bundled in our coats and scarves at the picnic table in my backyard, with cups of tea to keep us briefly warm.

Joan was born and raised in Athlone, in the center of the Republic of Ireland, the youngest of ten children in a devoutly religious Catholic family. Her father was in the Irish army, and more than one of his sons would follow him into the service. Military life led Tony, one of Joan's brothers, to whom she was especially close, to move to Letterkenny, and Joan started spending summers there as a teenager, and experienced a taste of freedom that was new to a girl who'd grown up beside the army barracks, who "felt like I had seven fathers, because I had six brothers." Unlike "civilian" kids in Letterkenny, there were no nights out at the disco for Joan, and those summers in Donegal gave her "a bigger sense of selfhood and independence." But, she said, "I made mistakes along the way."

She met a boy in Donegal and gave birth to her daughter, Naoimi, when she was nineteen. To be an unwed mother was still unacceptable in early '90s Ireland—"a shame on the family," as Joan put it, "what will the neighbors think? All this kind of carry-on."

The social pressure on unwed pregnant girls and women in

Ireland, until recently, cannot be overstated. The notorious Magdalene laundries—"mother and child" institutions usually affili-
ated with and overseen by Roman Catholic orders, once known as
repositories for so-called fallen women—separated mothers from
their babies, and effectively pressed the women into slave labor. As
Ann Marie Hourihane writes in *Sorry for Your Trouble: The Irish
Way of Death*:

> On entering the laundries the women, most of whom
> had had children out of wedlock, were treated as the
> most abject penitents. They had their hair hacked and
> their names changed, and they worked in the nuns'
> laundry business for no pay at all.

Could such a thing happen in our lifetime? It sounds like a
practice that must have ended in the nineteenth century. But the
last Magdalene laundry, Our Lady of Charity in Dublin, closed
in 1996, not long before Joan gave birth to her daughter. And it
might have taken even longer for the cruel institutions to be shut
down at last had it not been for the public outcry that followed the
discovery of a mass grave beside Dublin's Donnybrook laundry, in
which the remains of 155 women were discovered, unmarked, not
memorialized in any meaningful way—in any way at all.

The Magdalene laundries were not the only sites of confinement
and forced labor for unwed mothers and their children; there were
other workhouses, too, such as the one run by the Sisters of Bon
Secours in Tuam, County Galway. There, in 2017, according to
a BBC report, "children's remains were found in a mass grave in
an underground tank." A local historian, Catherine Corless, "had

spent months trying to find out why there were no marked graves for hundreds of the home's young residents. She had discovered death certificates for 796 Tuam children for whom there were no corresponding burial records." A chilling, infuriating, and heartbreaking state of affairs.

Twelve years before Our Lady of Charity shut down, a fifteen-year-old County Longford girl named Ann Lovett, who had concealed her pregnancy from her friends and family, died after giving birth in a grotto beside St. Mary's Church in her village, Granard. Her son was stillborn, and Ann died from a postpartum hemorrhage. She would have turned fifty in 2018—the year abortion was legalized in the Republic of Ireland by the repeal of the Eighth Amendment of the Constitution of Ireland, and the passing of the Thirty-eighth. Abortion was decriminalized in 2019 in Northern Ireland—it had been the last part of the United Kingdom to hold out—but access is severely limited.

The horror and grim sadness of all of this—the homes where "fallen women" were hidden away from "polite" society, their arduous unpaid labor, the unmarked, mass graves for women and children, the fear and shame and secrecy that would drive a teenage girl to her death—is more than enough to be, in itself, a dark and indelible stain on Ireland's history, particularly with respect to its treatment of women. In a public apology to the women of the Magdalene laundries, then-Taoiseach (head of the Irish government, equivalent to prime minister) Enda Kenny called the institutions "a national shame." It is also, at least on the surface, paradoxical, even hypocritical, that the deaths (and lives) of women and children would be so unvalued, and for so long, as to be unacknowledged, in a country known for its sensitivity to mourning and its rituals, for tending to and remembering and honoring and celebrating its dead.

I do not ask Joan if she considered abortion. That feels too personal, too fraught. Back in Brooklyn, my women friends (and some of my men friends) and I talked about abortion, it seemed, all the time—we were always up on news about reproductive health (and rights), we went to demonstrations, we offered up our bodies as shields at clinic defenses. But in this way my life here is very different: it's not a topic one raises in casual conversation, or even, in the case of my conversation with Joan, in more formal conversation. I can only surmise that abortion would have been even more objectionable to her religious family than unwedmotherhood, which in itself caused heavy consternation. So Joan married Naoimi's father—"the wrong man." Eighteen months later, their son, Matthew, was born. Within only a few weeks, "the wrong man" left his wife and their two young children.

"I was in dire straits," Joan says, and to support the family she worked full-time as a cleaner in a guest house. "It got to the stage where me and the kids were like the Three Musketeers—we ran the house together. I was young enough to enjoy them and be energetic with them, and we kind of grew up together." This closing of the ranks, tightening of the family circle, sounded familiar to me: my own mother often spoke the same way after my father left our family. It was just us, another trio of mother, son, and daughter—me, her, my brother, against the world. Three Musketeers.

"Matthew was very clever. Far cleverer than myself. He was my spell-check! He loved sports. He played Gaelic football and hurling, and soccer for a little while. He was so funny and lively, even up to his twenties. He was very childlike, very much a mammy's boy, you know, a typical Irish mammy and her son." She was happy to do Matthew's laundry, to shop and cook for him—to dote on him. In turn, he was protective, and loyal, and her stalwart cheerleader.

His twenties hadn't gotten off to a great start. His father and stepmother cut him out of their lives. He thought he'd gotten a girl pregnant—and was distraught when he heard the baby was stillborn (and later learned there hadn't been a baby at all). As young as he was, he looked forward to fatherhood, and had always told his mother that someday he would have loads of kids and live right next door to her and never leave. He adored children—and they loved him, too.

Because Matthew and Joan were so close, he was usually honest with his mother—but not always. What child is?

On an early August evening in 2013, he said he was going to a friend's house to play poker. "Don't be ringing me at three in the morning to pick you up," Joan told him. She expected to have an early, quiet night—and a drink or two, which would make driving out of the question for her. But Matthew wasn't going to a friend's house; he and some mates were going to a music festival a few towns away.

Sometime after two in the morning, Joan awakened to her cell phone ringing. "I'm like, thank you, Matthew, after telling you not to ring me! I'm not going to jump up and answer the phone straightaway. I let it go on for about half an hour before another message"—then another, and another. They were from one of his friends. Then, Joan thought, "Something's not right." There was something about *a car crash . . . I'm so sorry . . .*

The friend had witnessed the aftermath of the accident. He and other friends had come across it when they, too, were heading home from the festival, and all he could say was that he'd seen Matthew lying in the road. "We know it was Matthew because we know his runners," he told Joan. Matthew loved his trainers, as they usually call them here. He kept them neat and clean and shiny as new, lined up in an orderly row in his bedroom, which he also kept fastidiously tidy.

"I had this image in my head that my son had been thrown from this car and was lying on the road but I didn't know whether he was dead or alive, and was crying for his mama in the rain," Joan told me.

I had cursed the pandemic before, and at that moment I cursed it again. All I wanted to do was move closer to Joan, and hug her, at least put an arm around her. But COVID would not allow for comfort, for closeness, for a normal, necessary human response to personal tragedy.

Later, one of Matthew's close friends, Hayley, came to Joan's house. Together, they called the police and the hospitals. "I couldn't cope, so they took me to the *garda* station, and I remember those two young cops, and they were stalling and stalling, but you could see the looks. Eventually, they took me to the hospital."

When you enter the building, Joan explained, you turn left to go to the hospital, and right for the morgue. When the guards guided her to the right, Joan said, "Don't bring me down here, for God's sake, don't bring me down here. Just tell me is my son dead or alive."

"You have to tell *us*," a doctor said, "if this is your son."

I have steeled myself to identify bodies of dead loved ones, too.

In each instance, I felt both firmly planted to the hard floor of the morgue, but also not fully in my own body, my own mind, my own experience. I knew that I had a duty to perform, that I should collect myself, keep it together, get it done. But it also felt not real, as though it had to be an especially awful and lifelike nightmare. And then come the associations and observations: *She was seldom this still while she lived . . . Does he still look afraid . . . I can see the sweetness in his expression, the softness of his jawline . . .*

Joan shared a catalogue of her own memories and associations; they came quickly and vividly, and I was reminded of a book I love, Joe Brainard's beautiful and funny and unclassifiable memoir/poem/essay/artwork, *I Remember*, in which every single line begins with those two words. I have often used Brainard's approach as the basis for a writing exercise with my students—and it is an effective one. The memories pour forth, even for the most "blocked" writers, even for those most resistant to prompts, and most find it freeing. Joan might not think of herself as a gifted storyteller—in some ways, she underestimates herself—but she is.

"I remember walking in and he's lying on the slab and I'm looking at him like that, half his head covered in a cloth, and on the other half a massive black eye. I remembered when he was a boy, he'd fallen off a wall and gotten a black eye, and he was so proud of it, like it was a rite of passage. I remember looking up then thinking, you'd be so proud of that, son. It's a whopper." Her tone shifts, her shoulders tighten. "And then I saw all the hi-vis jackets, and told the police to get away from me."

. . . .

When I told my friend Brigid, before I moved to Glenarm, why I was making such a dramatic life change, she understood instantly. "If there is one thing we Irish know," Brigid, who was born and raised and lives in Belfast, wrote back, "it is how to bury our dead. We have had a great many centuries' practice." Of the North, in particular, she said, it is "a mournful, soulful, spiritual place in many ways and I mean that in a positive sense. We also know intimately what it is to mourn and keen over our beloveds."

Ireland is justly famous for many things: literature, drink, its patchwork landscape of greens, its pervasive sense of fun, its craic—and its distinctive response to death, dying, mourning, and (not) moving on—not so fast, anyway. The best-known expression of this distinctiveness is the tradition of the wake, about whose origins there are many theories, none of which are conclusive, and about which Hourihane writes:

> There is no strict definition of the Irish wake—it can refer to almost any social interaction associated with a death. But the classic image—open coffin in the middle of the room, mourners mirthfully toasting the dead— has deep roots in Irish culture. The old Irish wakes were carnivals and satires, they were talent competitions, they were matchmaking festivals (to put it politely) and they were fights. Catholic Church authorities spent centuries trying to suppress them . . . as late as 1927, the Synod of Maynooth felt it necessary to outlaw immodest behavior in the presence of a corpse.

But that, Hourihane continues, was antithetical to the very essence of the wake, its appeal, persistence, and necessity. "Immodest behaviours in the presence of a corpse were not a regrettable side effect of the Irish wake. They were exactly its point. It is a common impulse to laugh when you are frightened or upset, and in Ireland at least there is a strong instinct to party hard in the face of death."

Funerals are, of course, a big deal here, too. In June 2020, only a few months after COVID came to Northern Ireland, a well-known former IRA member and later Sinn Féin leader named Bobby Storey died at age sixty-four, after unsuccessful lung transplant surgery. Deep in that early lockdown, the number of mourners allowed at funerals in Northern Ireland was limited to twenty-five. An estimated one thousand mourners filled the streets for Storey's funeral procession in Belfast—including Sinn Féin's Michelle O'Neill, who was then deputy first minister of Northern Ireland, one of the joint heads of the government here.

For the first few months of the pandemic, I listened to BBC Radio Ulster's *The Nolan Show* almost every morning—even though it gave me headaches. It's a popular call-in program, and its host, Stephen Nolan, is a household name here—loved by some, reviled by others, listened to widely. It's loud and shouty, provocative and sometimes sensationalistic—the opposite of Brian Lehrer's show on New York's public radio station WNYC, to which I still listened most afternoons, especially in the early days of COVID, when Lehrer's gentle tone and calm, clear, intelligent presence felt like a balm during a terrible time, his voice one not only of reason, but of decency and empathy, too.

Over many mornings, many hours of heated discussion on *The Nolan Show* were devoted to Storey's funeral—and to Michelle O'Neill's presence there. I was riveted to this discussion, and to the responses of Nolan's callers. Although O'Neill had her defenders, mostly she was lambasted. Questions about to whom the rules and regulations of COVID restrictions applied persisted throughout the pandemic—usually with the appropriately indignant recognition that many of those who set the rules and make the laws, the people in power, expect one thing from their constituents (obedience) and another from themselves (exception). Not only were there strict limits on funeral attendance, there were also strict caps on the number of people allowed in cemeteries—and, indeed, many cemeteries were closed during the early lockdowns.

I remember one *Nolan Show* caller—angry, but more sad than angry—talking about the agony of not being permitted to visit a loved one's grave on his death anniversary, not being able to bring flowers, not being able to sit by the graveside, as she did every year on that day, with her memories, not being able to show the respect—and love—she had always shown before. That hundreds of mourners, including one of Northern Ireland's most prominent politicians, had crowded into Belfast's historic Milltown Cemetery to pay their respects to Bobby Storey, in disregard of the laws that "regular people" were expected to follow, only magnified her pain. I had been brought to Milltown Cemetery on a visit to the city in 2016, when my not-so-quietly Republican driver thought—"Because you're interested in history," he said—I should see the Republican plot where Bobby Sands and other IRA hunger strikers are buried, and I knew that my interest in history wasn't the only reason, or even the main one, he took me there.

It was important for him to remember these dead men, most of whom died so young, and for others to remember them, too.

I thought about how much it mattered to me to visit Frank's grave in Green-Wood Cemetery, in my old Brooklyn neighborhood, sometimes on his birthday and always on the anniversary of his death. How I'd made a ceremony of it: mixing a Manhattan—his favorite cocktail—in advance, to pour out for him on the ground under which the urn containing his ashes was interred, reading a poem by Wordsworth to him (could he hear it? somehow?), gently laying down a small bouquet of flowers or, in a pinch, a single rose from the nearest bodega. Afterward, I would walk to a neighborhood bar he loved, and where we'd both become friendly with the owner, David. And David would be waiting there, to make each of us a Manhattan—exactly the way Frank liked it—and to toast his memory together.

Even before I had lost some of those I loved most to death, graveyards mattered to me, and acted powerfully on my emotions. Long ago, without knowing that it would become a custom, I started to visit the graves of poets I admire: Robert Frost was first, his grave within walking distance of my college campus in Vermont—it was something we students did, one of our traditions, and I was surprised by how strongly I felt *something* when I went. Next was Emily Dickinson—a poet I love even more than Frost, much more—and I was nearly overcome. In Berlin, I sat beside Bertolt Brecht's final resting place and shocked myself by weeping—for all his sensitivity to human suffering, hardship, injustice, and pain, I don't imagine Brecht was much of a crier himself. In England, I have made many excursions to William Wordsworth's grave outside St. Oswald's Church in Grasmere, I have spent time in Winchester Cathedral with the remains of Jane Austen; I have found my way, with some effort, to John Milton's burial place in the magnificently named church of St. Giles without Cripplegate—right in the middle of an East London housing estate—and I have made myself a regular visitor to Bunhill Fields, where William Blake lies in eternity. In Rome, I have gazed upon the inscription—*Here lies one whose name was writ in water*—on John Keats's gravestone. At all of these places, whether I had sought it or not, I found closeness, and comfort.

But it is natural that the burial places of those we knew and loved affect us most of all. And in my experience of Ireland, cemeteries matter even more to the people here, as physical sites of love, grief, and remembrance. Mark's mother tends her own mother's grave, keeping it neat and bright with flowers. How strange it was, during those lockdowns, to walk by the cemeteries of Glenarm—the ancient and picturesque one at Saint Patrick's, by the sea, the newer one on the Straidkilly Road—and see them empty of people, no new flowers laid on graves, only old bouquets drying out, with no families gathered to honor their dead. Joan was ready to move away from Letterkenny and, like me, to try a new life in Glenarm. But the hardest part, she said, was "leaving Matthew behind." I understood this: although I felt more than ready to leave Brooklyn when I did, the thought that Green-Wood Cemetery, where both Frank and my mother are buried, would be so far away was painful to consider.

The day after Joan identified Matthew at the morgue, his body was brought back to her house—their home—for his wake. "I didn't want to have to go through all the pomp and ceremony, because I'd done that with mummy and daddy and Marion"—one of Joan's sisters, who died from cancer in 2002, and with whom she had been very close. "I just wanted my boy home." In the afternoon, she sent most of the family on their way, but let Matthew's friends come over that evening. "All of his mates came, and I told them this was their final night, that they would have a good party—Matthew was very social." Joan's brother David, a soldier, had prepared Matthew's clothing for the casket: "if there's one thing a soldier can do, they can iron."

Joan looked at her son in his casket, in his neatly pressed clothes. "I'm looking at him, and looking at him, going, '*This is not my boy, something's not right*,' and I realized he had no hair gel, and he would have always had his hair gelled. So I gently fixed it, and, yeah, it was kind of, '*there's* my Matthew.'" Exhausted, she crept upstairs to bed, and Naoimi joined her; they lay together quietly and fell asleep, knowing that Matthew was not alone downstairs, that his friends were still there with him. "I knew they would mind him and look after him," Joan remembers. They were the friends who had stuck by Matthew in his hardest times, and they would give him his final farewell, and Joan took comfort in that.

In mourning, comfort and despair come in waves, one overtaking the other. Sometimes grief has the quality of dreamtime about it, a floaty but certain sense that it occupies its own place, which requires its own way of living, and which is not quite attuned to the rhythms and events of "real" life in the "real" world. A court case followed Matthew's death, and it dragged on, as such things so often do, for more than two years—having the contradictory effect of simultaneously prolonging and postponing Joan's grief.

To appear at inquests, to pore over documents, to listen to the agonizing testimonies, Joan had to be present in real time, in the day-to-day. She would find no closure—a word against which I have often bristled when it appears in the context of loss—until the grinding machinations of the law finally switched off, and the case was closed. And she longed for closure. But I can tell that what Joan means by the word is different from the meaning I have associated with it and have resisted. That Joan might ever stop mourning her son was not possible, not thinkable, and she would not wish to stop mourning him. But she wanted justice, in as much as it could be served. And she wanted answers.

The image of her son lying in the middle of a dark road, crying out for her before dying, had tormented Joan since Matthew's death. It was not until the inquest, more than two years later, that she learned that what she had imagined did not match what had taken place. Matthew had been sitting in the front passenger seat with his seat belt on, and the high speed at which the oncoming car made impact caused him to bang his head against the glass window, hard. He died in the car, not on the road. Before the friend who had seen Matthew out there on the road, and knew him by his sneakers, had happened upon the accident, Matthew's body had been removed from the car and onto the road in order to get the other young men out of the back seat. It was still awful, still tragic—but knowing this gave Joan some relief; the worst, most pernicious and persistently haunting of her imaginings had not been true.

Joan told me about something else that had happened during the inquest that gave some comfort, too: the opportunity to tell the young man who, driving drunk, had killed Matthew that she did *not* forgive him.

Her admission of her unwillingness to forgive surprised me. It has become almost doctrine that forgiveness is not only virtuous and generous, it is also the right thing to do for oneself, the best balm for the troubled soul, a reliable and time-tested path to personal peace. I have listened to countless radio segments and watched hundreds of hours of daytime television devoted to confirming its healing power. A raft of self-help, New Age, and therapeutic books proclaims the good news of forgiveness—with titles and subtitles that describe it as freeing, a gift, a healer, even, in the language of the popular self-help author Eckhart Tolle, "radical." I would not dare to contradict the experiences of those who've found the granting of forgiveness meaningful and even transformative—Archbishop Desmond Tutu, for example, who coauthored *The Book of Forgiving: The Fourfold Path for Healing Ourselves and Our World* with his daughter, Mpho Tutu, would get no argument from me—but I have often wondered at the ways in which forgiveness seems to have turned into an industry of sorts, one that trades on human emotions, one that, to those of us who do not court it, can make us feel somehow deficient, coldhearted, emotionally inadequate. When we mourn, we often feel—and get signals from others—that we are somehow doing it wrong. There's an assumption that those of us whose loved ones died as a result of the actions of others can only find peace in forgiveness; this is another way in which the behavior of the bereaved is challenged, controlled, criticized, found lacking, unsophisticated, cold.

And yet, to some of us, like Joan, there is rightness, even

comfort, in not forgiving. To me, forgiveness has always felt too abstract even to understand. There is someone in my life who treated me badly when I was a child. We do not interact often, but she has sent clear messages, from time to time, that she wants, perhaps even expects, me to forgive her. I haven't, and I won't. And my refusal to forgive her does not have, as far as I can tell, any effect on me whatsoever, good or bad. Being unforgiving in this instance causes me no discomfort.

I have been encouraged by some people in my life to forgive myself for my absence at the moment of Frank's death, for not being by his side when I imagine he most wanted me there with him, needed me. I have tried to take this advice. I have even said aloud, "I forgive myself," repeating it like a chant, as one therapist advised me to do. It not only felt silly to me—and I can stomach quite a lot of silliness—it felt untruthful, and hollow, and, again, abstract. I cannot and will not forgive myself for that absence. I cannot will myself to "let go"—another thing many books about forgiveness allege that it promises. It does not feel honest. It does not feel like myself. Guilt is burdensome, uncomfortable, and sometimes ugly. But to live without it, or to think I can absolve myself of it at will, seems to deny some important dimension of my humanness, of the complex and imperfect story of myself.

My conversations with Joan made me think differently about mourning and loss. Her openness, her clarity, her attitude—all of these, in ways big and small, have challenged my own ways of thinking about, talking about, and coping with loss. They subvert a good deal of conventional wisdom. What she means by closure is not naively hopeful, unattainable, artificial, unrealistic. She knows its limits, and they do not extend to forfeiting her love and devotion to her son, or to subduing her expressions of them. Her unwillingness to forgive impressed me as honest, too, and even refreshing in its honesty.

In 2016, Joan and a friend took a holiday together to Spain, looking for nothing more than a change of scenery and a few days of fun—to get out of the norm, as she says, of life in Letterkenny, which had started to feel, since Matthew's death and the legal drama that followed it, more and more claustrophobic, like it was closing in on her. They randomly chose a pub. The barman clocked their Irish accents and said, "There's a boy down there from your country." Looking for love was the last thing on Joan's mind, but Stevey joined Joan and her friend, and the conversation flowed. Stevey took Joan's phone number—and called her later, he said, to make sure she'd given him the right number. They texted each other regularly for the next few days—and when both had returned to Ireland, he visited her in Letterkenny. Even then, Joan wasn't sure if this chance encounter in Spain would add up to something momentous.

He invited her to Glenarm—a place she'd never heard of, a place many people even here in Northern Ireland have never heard of. She'd never been to the Antrim Coast at all—her experiences in Northern Ireland had mostly been in Derry, not far from Letterkenny. While Stevey worked in the pub, Joan took walks in the forest and on the beach. "I'm not leaving this," she thought. "I don't feel the need to be numb."

It was after meeting Stevey and then coming to Glenarm that, Joan says, her grieving properly started: "that's when I really started to breathe." She believes that Matthew had a hand in that trip to Spain, that seemingly chance meeting in a pub. "There's a good man to look after you," she imagines her son—who'd never liked any of her romantic partners—saying about Stevey. "He'll look after you, and he'll make life better, and it might be in totally unknown territory in a new place." And in this unknown territory, like me, Joan has discovered a peace that she could not grasp in Letterkenny, that I could not get in New York City. She has made good friends here, and found acceptance—more than acceptance, love.

When we met in 2017, it was Joan who first described Glenarm to me as "a healing place." And when she did, I sensed that she was right, and that I should find out for myself if it might help to heal me, too.

13

EARLY 2021: MIDWAY BETWEEN THE WINTER SOL-
stice and the vernal equinox, between the darkest and shortest day
and the burgeoning life and sunlight of spring—a hopeful crossroads, the start of something new. It is February 1, the feast day of
Saint Brigid—that great and godly woman who could turn water
into whiskey—and in Glenarm it is damp and gray and cold but
it's also vibrating with goodness and anticipation: there are already
snowdrops and early tulips poking up through the hard soil. The
days are lengthening; I can feel it.

It is also the ancient, pre-Christian Celtic festival of Imbolc, a
day to be hopeful, when the doorway to brighter times, more light,
begins to crack itself open. Imbolc's etymology isn't known for
sure, but might be from the Old Irish for "in the belly," or an even
older word for "budding," or possibly from "ewe's milk." In all
cases, it is nothing if not pregnant—nourishing and new, all promise and potential. Unlike September 11, when I arrived in Glenarm
to stay for a while. Unlike Valentine's Day, which I had resisted
until Frank and I had stumbled on a way to make it matter, which
retreated again after he died.

Right, there's that, too: February 1 is when the month I hate most begins, a month whose only kindness is its brevity. Frank died in February. Ma died in February. My uncle Bill, my cat: they died in February. Most years since Frank's death, I have awakened on this day and said, *February, go fuck yourself.*

But this February 1 was different.

For Mark and me, it was also our wedding day.

It wasn't our first choice. We had planned to marry the previous November, on Thanksgiving—a holiday I love, as much as I detest its colonialist origins. But when I gathered my most important documents in a folder to bring with me from New York, the one I couldn't find was my birth certificate, and in the middle of a pandemic, it took months to get one from the New York City Department of Health. Without my birth certificate, we couldn't get a marriage license. I had found Frank's death certificate, which I thought I might need someday, but couldn't imagine what for. I needed it for a new marriage license, too.

While we waited for my birth certificate to arrive, Mark, with his usual optimism, had gone ahead and booked the Barbican—the castle gatehouse where we stayed when we first came to Glenarm five years before—for a late November honeymoon a three-minute walk from our house, but still a welcome change of scenery, still romantic, sentimental in the best way. It would be a return to the place where we fell in love with Glenarm, and started to fall in love with each other. The visit when Mark made me soup, bought me crackers and ginger ale, took the bus back to Glenarm after a long day's work in Belfast to make sure that I was okay and not alone. And that's when I thought, maybe this man is more than my fixer in Ulster, and more than a friend, when I learned he is a good caregiver, and that he can cook. Early days: still a long time before I ever imagined him as *husband*.

When we chose to isolate together in March 2020, I started calling him my co-quarantinee. But I knew by then he was more than that, even if I was afraid to say it.

We went backward into our married life, with our honeymoon more than two months before our wedding, and nothing about that felt wrong in the mixed-up, *what-is-time-anyway?* time that the pandemic had imposed on us all. At the Barbican, we ate Thanksgiving dinner, played cards by the fire as we had in 2016, and left our laptops at home; there was still no Wi-Fi in the tower, and no television. We retired our phones to an end table and talked. On the last day it had felt safe to be in Belfast, I bought a book of Chekhov's stories, and I read one to Mark, then he read one to me. Two sad stories of marriages that did not thrive: "The Huntsman," in which a husband and wife, estranged for twelve years, have a harrowing, chance encounter, and "About Love," whose narrator concludes that when you love someone, "your reasoning about that love should be based on what is supreme, on what is more important than happiness or unhappiness, sin or virtue." Maybe I had once believed that, or something like it. For a long time, happiness had been turning into something that seemed more and more abstract, so slippery as to seem unattainable. I remembered joking, or half-joking, whenever friends said I *seemed* happy, that "happiness was beside the point." I made light of it, I pretended it was distasteful, as though happiness is too simple, too easy, too selfish. But what I really questioned was if I deserved it.

I thought about how my mother answered the question "How

are you?" with "*Compared to whom?*," which was so funny and so sad, and I remembered her remembering herself as an aspiring young actress doing Chekhov in drama school: *I am in mourning for my life.*

That was how she had lived, for so many years, after my parents' marriage ended. And if there is a difference between grief and mourning, and I know there is—grief is what we feel after the greatest losses, mourning is how we enact that grief, in public and to ourselves—I too had been mourning for a long time. Unhappiness felt like a badge, one that I had both inherited and earned. And now, after so many years of resisting it, feeling unworthy of it, even belittling it, it felt like there might be nothing greater I could ask of love than happiness—not something supreme, idealized, impossible.

When I left Brooklyn for Glenarm, I knew that the act of relocation in itself would not quell all my anxieties about work, money, relationships, and health. I knew that depression, my tricky and steadfast companion since adolescence, would not lift up like a fallen leaf and blow away. I knew that Brexit was on its way, and with it old tensions might reawaken, and the fragile peace the North had known since the Troubles ended might falter. But my heart longed for the sea and the forest, for the spirit of this place and its people, and the forces that drew me here were too strong to resist. Moving would not "fix" me, but another way of living, here, in this quiet and healing place, might start to heal me, too. A few years later, after so much has happened, after learning so much from friends and neighbors here, my instincts were not wrong: this place has a magic of its own, and if I was open to it, it would lead to possibilities I hadn't dared to consider—especially, the possibility of happiness.

A few days before our wedding, Mark and I gave ourselves haircuts; hair salons had reopened intermittently during the pandemic, but I was reluctant to visit one. I painted my toenails for the first time in more than a year—a bright, bloomy pink tinged with orange. I wore a long, bright pink dress with enormous roses printed on it—a dress I had previously worn on May Days in Brooklyn, to celebrate another favorite holiday with pagan roots. I braided and pinned up my hair, and put on a golden headband, like a small and subtle tiara, that was a gift from Brigid. I had turned fifty a few weeks before the big day.

Mark had been discreet about the black damask waistcoat he'd ordered for the occasion, and I loved both the secrecy and his new garment, which he wore with black jeans, a buckle with a big pewter bat in the middle, and the flowered, deep blue shirt I'd given him for Christmas. I ordered a bouquet from a florist in Larne, recommended by my friend Mona—a spray of early spring flowers and grasses, in soft yellows and greens and muted purples. Mark had already, on our engagement, given me a Claddagh—the traditional Irish ring bearing a heart cradled by two hands, that represents love and loyalty. I wore it with the heart facing outward until our wedding day, when he would return it to my ring finger with the heart facing inward. We were ready to get married, and we looked it.

When I told friends back in New York about our engagement, like us, they had dreamy, pastoral visions of our wedding, and so did we: what could be more romantic than a wedding in the Irish countryside, in the village we loved? But the ceremony we'd envisioned—in the forest, by the river, with a small circle of loved ones gathered around us, followed by a big party at Stevey's, for anyone who wanted to come (the whole village, we hoped)—was not to be. Quickly changing COVID rules forced us to revise our plans.

We were married in the Larne registrar's office—a good contender for Least Romantic Place in All of Ireland, in a good contender for the Least Romantic Town. (Mark prefers to tell people we got married in Ulfreksfjord—the old name for Larne when it was the only Viking settlement on the Antrim Coast.) Larne. The place with the biggest July 11 bonfire. Larne—whose bus station on a cold Sunday evening is just about the loneliest place I've ever been.

No matter: we were still thrilled. We were allowed to have up to nine guests, but we played it safe and settled on four: Mark's mother and youngest sister, Jo, were there, and Brigid and Róisín came from Belfast to be there as our friends but also, I think, to stand in for my side of the family. We all wore masks, which by then didn't feel as unnatural to us as they might have felt a few months earlier. A masked wedding. In Larne.

And there we were, in a conference room whose décor seemed unchanged since the 1980s, under a portrait of Queen Elizabeth II. Rhonda, the registrar, was a warm and easeful celebrant, not stiff and officious at all. And just as there had been gaffes leading up to our wedding—that birth certificate, a ring that had to be reordered and resized—there were some during the ceremony, too. Other friends and family members were watching on Zoom: someone forgot to turn their microphone off, and we could hear chatter in the background. I dropped Mark's ring to the floor before sliding it onto his finger (many people who watched us on Zoom said that was their favorite part). With only our small wedding party, we were still surrounded by love, and we could feel it.

In the registry office parking lot, the six of us had cake and champagne out of the trunk of Mark's sister's car, toasted, and took photographs. Jo drove us home, and as Mark and I crossed the threshold again into the home we had already shared for almost a year, something felt different. No longer just friends, no longer co-quarantinees, we were spouses now, who loved each other, who had made vows and exchanged rings.

We built a fire in the living room. There were friendly knocks on our door throughout the evening: friends in the village gave us gifts of champagne, and one baked us a wedding cake to our specifications: a carrot cake, dressed up with pistachios and orange zest—exactly what we wanted, simple and homey and delicious. She even loaned us her beautiful porcelain cake plate and knife. We cooked ourselves a wedding dinner of duck breasts in port sauce, potatoes dauphinoise, and sauteed greens. We toasted ourselves and each other with champagne. We ate our perfect cake. We fell asleep early, in our house, in our village, mister and missus.

Since that day in Larne, I have sometimes wondered if marrying again means that I am no longer a widow. I have concluded that it does not—even if every form that asks me to confirm my relationship status makes me check a box that says that it does. I am married, but I will always be a widow. I will find ways to look forward, with Mark, while remembering all that has come before.

I no longer feel that I am in mourning for my own life, but I continue to observe rituals of mourning and remembrances for my loved ones who have died, especially Frank and my mother. They will always matter to me, and Mark understands that. On the anniversary of Frank's death, I still make a Manhattan and raise the glass to him. On my mother's, I look at the photographs of her I brought with me, which remind of all that was good and rare in her: her humor and wit, her style and beauty, her easy smile, her love for animals. I do these things because I believe that they longed to be remembered, that we all do, and because these rituals both honor those I've lost and give me comfort.

I still hear my mother's voice, and still have conversations with her, especially when I cook, which is our time together. She'd be amazed to see some of the things I get up to in my Glenarm kitchen.

Ma, I've cooked more Jewish food in a few years here than I cooked in a lifetime in New York City. I make a pretty nice challah. I make the best matzo balls in Ireland—maybe the world. The secret is goose fat. I make my own bagels now and they're like the ones you had when you were a kid in Brooklyn—smallish and chewy and dense.

Ma, can you believe that Chinese restaurants here don't have dumplings? It's criminal. I've gotten good at those, too. Pork and chives and cabbage. The key is very fatty pork.

Ma, my fried chicken won't ever be as good as yours, but I keep trying.

This is a good place. I'm happy here. And you'd love Mark. You two would crack each other up.

I no longer have that strange feeling that had stalked me for so long—that I was having experiences that had been meant for Frank, and that I had been given opportunities that should have been his. I no longer feel guided—or haunted—by him. I still wish I had been with him when he died, but I have surrendered the notion that by breaking his heart, I caused his death. I do not see any of this as a letting-go: I still want to hold him in my thoughts, carry him in my heart. On Valentine's Day, I still read portions of the poem that had been ours.

When I think about him now, I close my eyes and I can still see the distinctive tilt of his head when something puzzles him, or falls on his ears as improbable, disingenuous, wrong. Frank, these last few years would have given you so many head-tilting opportunities. I don't have conversations with him the way I do with my mother, but if I did, this is what I'd tell him:

I sure wish you hadn't died.

But the Trump presidency might have killed you had you lived long enough.

And let's not even get into COVID.

I love you. Rest.

After the wedding, I applied for a family visa. The process isn't easy: it is an expensive, debilitating, often demoralizing undertaking that taught me that I hadn't shed my instinctive pessimism—and that I desperately wanted to stay in Glenarm. I prayed. I cried. I took long walks. I was tightly wound, and overcome by worries that my application might be denied because of some stupid thing or other I'd done in the past, some mistake I'd made, my debt, my activism, the publications I wrote for, my Communist uncle, something. Ghosts showed up every day to remind me—in case I'd forgotten—what a fuckup I was, and that if I didn't get a visa it was nobody's fault but my own.

I was the most depressed I'd felt since I moved to Glenarm. After many months on a long NHS waiting list, I returned to therapy for the first time in almost a decade. I met with my therapist once a week on Zoom. My eight sessions with Carolyn might have the makings of a sitcom: the Jewish patient from New York, the lapsed Catholic mental health care professional from the Glens of Antrim.

"I've never had a patient quite like you," she said one day, with a smile.

"And Carolyn, I've never had a therapist quite like *you*."

In the Glens of Antrim, even the therapy is good craic. But as much as she and I amused each other—every appointment had at least a few good laughs—it was clear that she was serious about her work, and that I was serious about needing help. And those weekly conversations did help me.

I trembled every morning when I logged on to my email. When my visa application was approved, I cried some more. I had imagined packing up another home, leaving Glenarm, leaving Mark, leaving the life together we had only just begun. I was so glad I could stay, and so grateful I considered kissing the rich brown earth in Glenarm Forest.

The day after my visa was approved, I started poring over animal rescue websites, looking for a nice senior dog to adopt, to give him or her a comfortable retirement by the sea. It was the longest I'd gone without a pet in my life, but to adopt one before I knew I could stay here for the long haul would have been unfair, if not cruel. I hadn't lived with a dog since I was a teenager, and had spent all of my adult life in Brooklyn in the company of cats. But Glenarm isn't just paradise to me—it's a dog's paradise, too.

The first summer during the COVID pandemic, a beautiful fox red Labrador named Ruby, who belonged to the Boyle family just up the road on Altmore Street, gave birth to a litter of ten pups. The Boyles' house is on the way to the forest, and right next to the honesty box where I bought fresh eggs from Jordan, the gardener and beekeeper at Glenarm Castle. The Boyles let the puppies play in their gated front yard during the day, and I found myself buying more eggs than usual so I could catch a glimpse of the babies at play. But there was no need for subterfuge: the Boyles were happy to let passersby sit on their fence and pet the dogs, hold them, hug them. The puppies became local celebrities—I think even people from nearby villages made the trip to see them—and brought unencumbered joy to Glenarm. How I wanted to scoop one up and take her home! But I had no business getting a dog before I had a clear picture of where I might be a few months later.

When the time to get a dog arrived, I kept returning to one page on one rescue site, describing an eleven-year-old Jack Russell terrier named Milo. The photograph was a blurry partial profile shot, awkwardly cropped and out of focus; I couldn't tell what he looked like. But I didn't care: the shelter described him as "a little gem," a quiet and settled boy "who loves his walks and always has a wag of his little tail." I don't believe in fate, or that the universe is anything but indifferent to us. But I knew he was the dog for us. I texted his picture to Mark at work. "Let's get Milo," he said. Seventeen days later, after two visits to the shelter and a home inspection, we took him to Glenarm. Now he's the center of our lives, our in-house comedian, protector, prince of love, and muse. He has made us a family. A little gem, for sure—and, as Jacky observed when they first met, "He's got a real life force about him."

He may have been quiet during his stay at the shelter, but in our home he found his voice—and uses it. And that photograph on the website did not do him justice: he is athletic and handsome, soulful and proud—to my eyes, like a dog right out of a Stubbs painting.

When vaccinations became more available, and travel less onerous, friends from New York who'd planned to visit me in 2020 started arriving. I couldn't wait to show off Glenarm to them: to walk with them in the forest, and on the shore. To show them the Barbican—where it all started, at least for me. To treat them to a pint or an Irish coffee at Stevey's. To take them to the walled garden, which always makes me feel like my hero Dickon, in *The Secret Garden*. My pride in this place feels good—and so does seeing it freshly through my friends' eyes. So far, they all get it, they all get Glenarm, the town that time forgot. I expect they'll all come back. Now that it looks like I'll be staying awhile, I hope so.

When one friend returned to Brooklyn, she shared some photos she'd taken in the forest, and said, "Thank you for sharing your beautiful life with me, Rosie, Mark, and Milo."

It *is* a beautiful life.

It is not a perfect life, but it is a beautiful life.

I did not leave New York because I was "over it." I can't imagine getting over New York. But I knew if I didn't listen to my heart and follow my instincts, I might never move to Ireland. I will always love New York. But I don't think I could live there again. I have returned once, and briefly, for my cousin Phil's memorial service. Death had driven me from New York, and it had brought me back. The night before my flight to JFK, I stayed in Belfast with Brigid. As we did the dishes after dinner, she asked me about my return flight. "I leave New York on Friday night," I told her, "and I'll be home on Saturday afternoon."

"That's the first time I've heard you refer to *here* as home," she said.

"I guess that means it *is* home now."

My week in New York was bewildering. After two years in Glenarm, I no longer felt like a city person—I'd become a real *culchie* as we say in Northern Ireland, a bumpkin. My cousin's memorial service was the reason for my trip, but I fit in as many visits with friends as I could, and an overnight stay in Connecticut with my brother, his wife, and their kids. I also stuffed my face with soup dumplings, New York pizza, and other foods I'd missed.

But nothing felt more New York to me than pacing the aisles

of a big Duane Reade pharmacy on lower Broadway, looking for a bottle of Advil and a tube of Neosporin to take back to Glenarm. As I was leaving the store, a friendly man who was panhandling nearby sized me up and said, "Hey, you're a *real* New Yorker." Then he started singing Odyssey's 1977 disco hit "Native New Yorker" to me.

For a minute, I swelled with pride. Yes, I may have left this town, but I'm a *real* New Yorker, a *native* New Yorker, and it shows. I still got it. I gave the man five dollars.

It wasn't until I was three blocks away that I remembered I had a *New Yorker* magazine tote bag slung over my shoulder.

No, I hadn't moved to Glenarm because I was over New York. I moved to Glenarm because it had captured my heart and my imagination, and because I had a feeling that, here, my experience of grieving would transform. Before I met Jacky, before I heard Joan describe the village as a healing place, I sensed that it was. My instincts, this time, were right.

There are nuances to the Irish response to death and grief, of course. As my friend Brigid told me long ago, they know how to bury their dead. And how to remember, and celebrate them, too. But I also know—from the old and not-so-old tales of isolated and feared widows, from the heartbreaking stories of the Magdalene laundries and makeshift mass graves—that even here, where death is spoken of so naturally and so often, not every person who lived and then died has been given his or her due. Not every person has been shown compassion, nor is remembered with love and tenderness. Ireland has not been faultless in the face of death.

But its special intimacy with death and grief, and its normalization of loss is still widespread all over the island, and I mean this as a compliment. The eye contact, the willingness to listen, and listen well, to the stories of others' suffering: I experience, and benefit, from all of this almost every day.

Living here has transformed the way I grieve: what I had hoped for was not only a way to live with it, but to live *in* it—without giving it the authority to define or limit me. And Glenarm has given that to me: this village that seemed itself to be dying, where memorials appear on woodland walks, in seaside graveyards, and, most of all, in the stories that my neighbors here have shared with me, with grace.

I used to bristle whenever anyone accused me of cynicism. I'd correct them and say I wasn't a cynic, I was a pessimist. Terrible things do happen, I'd remind them. We bear witness to trauma and pain and devastation every day: in the newspapers we read, in the stories we hear, sometimes in our own homes, and often in our hearts. Terrible things do happen, and they may as well happen to us. Pessimism had become my shield: if I kept my expectations low, and believed that the worst was always possible, it was harder to be disappointed, or bitter.

But I know now that I was both a pessimist and a cynic. When I stopped believing that wonder was still possible in my life, I dismissed it as childish and corny. (And I admit that even typing the word "wonder" still makes me cringe, but I'm getting there.) When happiness no longer felt like something I deserved, I wrote it off as an abstraction, and a shallow one, and made instead a virtue of sadness.

When I started writing this book, I could not foresee how my time here would unfold. I did not know how long I'd stay—a year, I thought, maybe a little more. I did not foresee a wedding. Or a dog. And I also didn't have a title.

I wanted to call it "North"—but Seamus Heaney beat me to it, and you can't compete with Seamus Heaney ever, but especially when you're writing about the North.

So I looked to his poetry. When people—especially politicians—talk about Northern Ireland, they often quote these lines from Heaney's "The Cure at Troy":

> It means once in a lifetime
> That justice can rise up
> And hope and history rhyme.

But these lines struck a clearer chord for me, and you'll see why:

> Believe that a further shore
> Is reachable from here. Believe in miracles
> And cures and healing wells.

Healing wells! He might have been writing about Glenarm, not Troy. And "A Further Shore" sounded like a perfect title for a book about grief and loss—and moving to Northern Ireland.

But that wouldn't do, either: Gerry Adams had written a book called *A Farther Shore*. And no other lines or phrases I came across in Heaney's—or Ciaran Carson's, or Michael Longley's, or Sinéad Morrissey's, or any other great Northern poet's—work felt right.

Instead, I confess, I stole the title from the Glenarm Tourism website, which draws its viewers in with this opening line: "Glenarm is full of charm and beauty on the slow road to the Causeway Coast." So I didn't exactly steal it, I adapted it to "The Slow Road North." But it still felt a little dirty. I told myself it was only a working title, a placeholder until the real title came to me. But nothing came to me.

One night I called my friend Katherine, the same Katherine I'd been with over that blissful weekend at Magherintemple Lodge outside Ballycastle, when I was reporting the Roger Casement story. She's not only a dear friend, she's a terrific writer. She had also been my editor long ago, when I wrote a few stories for Al Jazeera America's website—and she's one of the best editors I've ever had. She's always got smart ideas, a fresh perspective, a clear and critical eye. She'd be just the right person to brainstorm with me, and help me find a title.

"So what's the problem?" she asked me over Zoom.

"My book needs a title."

"Does it have a working title?"

"It does."

"Well?"

I told her the working title was "The Slow Road North," and that I'd lifted it from Glenarm's tourist center's website, and I didn't feel great about it.

She liked it.

And when she asked me why I didn't, I paused and had to think about it. My issue, I realized, was the word "road." To me, it came a little too close to "journey," which, like "wonder," had long been a word that made me roll my eyes. Why had everything become a *journey*? (The cynicism I never saw when it afflicted me is so visible to me now.)

"But you *have* been on a journey," Katherine said. "And grief is a slow road. And you did move north."

She was right. She's always right.

Grief has been a slow road, and as long as I continue to live and to love others, I have not reached its end. But Glenarm is more than a way station on this *journey*. It is where my grief and I have made our home, in this place of cures and healing wells.

Epilogue

LIKE MANY RURAL VILLAGES IN IRELAND AND ELSE-where, Glenarm has seen many changes, big and small, since COVID came along. I'd estimate that when I first set eyes on this place in 2016, about half a dozen properties were up for sale on Toberwine, the main street. As I write this, there are two—and only one other is on the market elsewhere in the village. Picturesque country villages have become more attractive to city dwellers—and having lived here through the worst of the pandemic (and as a longtime city dweller myself), I understand why.

And after years of inertia, other changes are afoot in the village: there are new restrooms beside the beach promenade, the formerly derelict Eglinton Yard (once a cigarette plant, later a furniture factory, among its many long-ago uses) has been refurbished into a multipurpose community space. A long-awaited restaurant will soon open. And I should warn you that, due to factors beyond Stevey's control, the price of a pint of Guinness has gone up to £4—still a bargain, still the best you'll ever taste.

Change brings hope—along with some new worries. Will local families be displaced by rising property prices? Will Glenarm—

regarded by some as a hidden gem, a well-kept secret, and by others as a forgotten place—become the vibrant, bustling place it once was, or maybe even too popular for its own good? It is still too early, I think, to know.

When I moved to Glenarm in 2019, the implementation of Brexit loomed—and I expected that it would be the major topic of conversation in the village's pubs and living rooms. It was not (and was decisively upstaged by COVID six months later). Most people here, it seemed, were already talked out on the subject, a process from which many had felt disenfranchised from the start; more than 55 percent of Northern Irish voters voted to remain in the EU. And those voters, along with everyone else in the North, have felt Brexit's effects in the prolonged nonexistence of a functioning government, without which major decisions about crucial issues, such as health care, could not be made.

Brexit's effects are unfortunately present in other, more local ways, too. The Glenarm I visited in 2016—and, remember, I first came here during July 12, when tensions are likelier to boil over than at any other time—had little on display in the way of flags and other sectarian signage. That's changed: Union Jacks are in abundance for many weeks during the year—a result, I think, of Brexit's emboldening of certain Loyalist factions. Some smaller marches in the village have taken on a more hostile tenor. It is still a peaceful and lovely place to live—but, to me anyway, subtly different.

One of the questions I've had in the forefront of my mind since I started writing this book is this: how did Glenarm go from being a thriving village, abundant in shops and services and people, to a place written off as forgotten, if not dead? In most of my conversations with people here, the Troubles, which I believed to be the likeliest culprit, were not offered as an explanation, and I did not ask leading questions about those terrible times, reluctant to open old wounds and do harm. Most people I spoke with attributed the village's decline to familiar, if not universal, causes of small-town regression: people leaving to seek more (and better) opportunities for work, mom-and-pop shops failing in the face of big supermarkets and department stores in larger towns nearby, small industrial employers like factories and mills becoming obsolete (or moving production to some far-away elsewhere).

I do not doubt that these factors all played roles in Glenarm's story. But I also believe that the Troubles figured more urgently into Glenarm's fortunes than most people are willing to say. There were, I know, families who moved—or who sent their children to live with relatives in England, the Republic of Ireland, Canada, and Australia—to circumvent the violence, and to avoid forced indoctrination by paramilitaries to stay alive.

I am not suggesting that many of the people who shared their stories and insights with me were being dishonest. I am also not suggesting that they are gripped by a kind of selective, collective amnesia—of the sort, for example, my brother, a student of World War II history, faced in Lyon when he asked locals if they might direct him to the Hotel Terminus, the seat of the Vichy regime, and was repeatedly told they had no idea what he was talking about. What I believe is that the reticence I often encountered on the subject of the Troubles is a reflection of the trauma those years inflicted upon the people here—that, for many, it is too sensitive and painful to discuss, too unhappy to recollect at will.

Mark and I had known each other for more than a decade, and

had been married for more than a year, when, for example, he first mentioned to me that his grandmother's home in Armagh had been firebombed. To me, it seemed like an event too terrible, too huge, to have withheld; to him, it was not a thing to dwell upon—what mattered, he has often said, was getting on with it, getting on with life, because, really, what else could one do?

I am amazed by so many of the people I have come to know here, particularly those of my own generation and older, who lived through the very worst of it. That they are still standing, still getting on with it, is enough to make me admire them. That they do it with so much humor and wit, warmth and generosity, astounds me.

Acknowledgments

THIS BOOK PASSED THROUGH MANY CAPABLE HANDS on its slow road to publication, and was shown genial hospitality at many stops along the way. I am indebted to three talented editors for their sharp minds and kind spirits: Susan Canavan, Emma Effinger, and Pilar Garcia-Brown. At Waxman Literary Agency, I thank Ashley Lopez and Scott Waxman for being so exceptionally good at what they do.

My thanks to Steve Reddicliffe, the editor who said yes to my Roger Casement pitch, when neither of us had any idea that reporting that story would change my life. Gratitude is also due to Sari Botton—editor of the revised edition of the essay collection *Goodbye to All That: Writers on Loving and Leaving New York*, in which an earlier version of chapter 4 appeared under the title "Homemaker."

Two brilliant, warm, and wise Belfast women—Brigid Loughran and her daughter, Róisín Davis—have become like family to me here in the North, and one could not find better kin, or better craic, anywhere. My thanks, too, to the brilliant, warm, and wise Dublin contingent: Rosita Boland and Nicole Rourke.

As a student at the Seamus Heaney Centre at Queen's University Belfast, I shared the earliest iterations of some other chapters and benefitted from feedback from my classmates and lecturers. Felix McKillop kindly loaned me a copy of his indispensable book, *Glenarm: A Local History*. Storyteller and writer Liz Weir directed me to dúchas.ie, the mind-blowing online home of the Irish National Folklore Collection. Willa Murphy rekindled my love for Mary Lavin.

I never would have made it to Glenarm in 2019 without the support and generosity of my friends and family. I am especially grateful to Jami Attenberg, Lucy Duba, Melanie Dunea, the Eichleay family, Ruth Franklin, Katie Freeman, Marc Gilman and Estee Pierce, Jeff Gordinier, Laurie Gunst, Jean Holabird, Lee McElfresh, Laura McKellar, Katherine Lanpher, Winter Miller, Maya Perkins, Maggie Ruggiero, Jeremy Schaap, Nancy and Joe Silvio, Jane Teller, Sophie Weber, and the Jaffe family.

My greatest debt is to the people of Glenarm, particularly those who have shared their insights and entrusted me with their stories: Joan Crawford, Jacky Geary, Mona Hyndman, Ashleigh Moran, Colin Urwin, and Frances Wilson and her husband, Jackie—whose death in 2022 was a profound loss. Many other friends and neighbors here have also been supportive in invaluable ways, including Hillary and William Cross, Floresca Karanasou and Paul Lalor, Wendy Lindbergh and Hector McDonnell, Maureen McAuley, Stevey McAuley, Penny and Dennis McBride, Sue McBride, Greer and James McNally, Jenny and Pete Monroe, Charlene Wilson—and all my fellow members of the village's spirited book club and the mighty Glenarm Wildlife Group.

ACKNOWLEDGMENTS

Mark and Milo, you madmen, I love you: your optimism tempers my pessimism, your hopefulness softens my gloom, and your humor lifts me up every day. Thank you for making such a funny wee family with me in our beautiful and beloved village.

Works Cited

Carson, Ciaran. *Belfast Confetti*. Winston-Salem, NC: Wake Forest University Press, 1989.

Education Authority website, www.eani.org.uk.

Gartland, Fiona. "Winged Messenger of Solace—An Irishwoman's Diary on the Robin Redbreast." *The Irish Times*, July 17, 2017.

Gordon, Mary. "Mary Lavin and Writing Women." *American Journal of Irish Studies*, vol. 10, 2013.

Heaney, Seamus. *The Cure at Troy: A Version of Sophocles' Philoctetes*. New York: Farrar, Straus and Giroux, 1991.

Hourihane, Ann Marie. *Sorry for Your Trouble: The Irish Way of Death*. Dublin: Sandycove, 2021.

Joyce, James. "The Dead." In *Dubliners*. London: Grant Richards Ltd., 1914.

Joyce, Patrick Weston. *English as We Speak It in Ireland*. London: Longmans, Green and Co. 1910.

Lavin, Mary. *In the Middle of the Fields*. Dublin: New Island, 2016. Introduction by Colm Tóibín.

McBride, Jack. *Traveller in the Glens*. Belfast: Appletree Press, 1979.

McKillop, Felix. *Glenarm: A Local History*. Self-published, 1987.

Patterson, Glenn. "Don't Mention the C Word." *The Irish Times*, January 4, 2014.